*"Twenty-volume folios
will never make a revolution.
It's the little pocket pamphlets
that are to be feared."*
Voltaire

FIELD (#7) **NOTES**

DEBORAH DUNDAS

ON CLASS

BIBLIOASIS
Windsor, Ontario

FIRST EDITION
10 9 8 7 6 5 4 3 2 1

Library and Archives Canada Cataloguing in Publication
Title: On class / Deborah Dundas.
Names: Dundas, Deborah, author.
Series: Field notes (Biblioasis) ; #7.
Description: Series statement: Field notes ; #7
Identifiers: Canadiana (print) 20220255865 | Canadiana (ebook) 20220255997
    ISBN 9781771964814 (softcover) | ISBN 9781771964821 (ebook)
Subjects: LCSH: Social classes—Canada. | LCSH: Poverty—Canada. | LCSH:
    Poor—Canada.
Classification: LCC HN103.5 .D86 2022 | DDC 305.50971—dc23

Edited by Daniel Wells
Copyedited by Rachel Ironstone
Typeset by Vanessa Stauffer
Series designed by Ingrid Paulson

Canada Council for the Arts   Conseil des Arts du Canada

ONTARIO ARTS COUNCIL
CONSEIL DES ARTS DE L'ONTARIO
an Ontario government agency
un organisme du gouvernement de l'Ontario

Canada

ONTARIO | ONTARIO
CREATES | CRÉATIF

Published with the generous assistance of the Canada Council for the Arts, which last year invested $153 million to bring the arts to Canadians throughout the country, and the financial support of the Government of Canada. Biblioasis also acknowledges the support of the Ontario Arts Council (OAC), an agency of the Government of Ontario, which last year funded 1,709 individual artists and 1,078 organizations in 204 communities across Ontario, for a total of $52.1 million, and the contribution of the Government of Ontario through the Ontario Book Publishing Tax Credit and Ontario Creates.

PRINTED AND BOUND IN CANADA

Contents

Introduction

IN APRIL 2020, Lise Hewak drove to her job as a cashier at a local grocery store in Guelph, Ontario. She'd only worked there since November, picking up the part-time gig after retiring early from her profession as an occupational therapist. Things had changed mightily in just a few months. The Covid-19 pandemic had driven the province of Ontario into lockdown on March 13, requiring everyone who could work from home to stay there. Schools turned to virtual learning, and we scrambled to find masks to protect ourselves and others as we cautiously went out to do basic shopping and stockpiled toilet paper, flour, and yeast.

With an echo of the postal worker's creed—*neither rain nor sleet nor snow nor pandemic*—essential workers, including doctors and nurses, personal support workers caring for seniors, and retail employees, masked up and went to work. Everyday heroes we called them. For a short time, some grocery stores, including the one Lise works for, increased the wages of their front-line workers and called it hero pay; personal support workers were given a wage boost too.[1] Our lives depended on them, after all.

We embraced our communities and the idea that we were all in this together. We went on our front porches and balconies or leaned out windows, from Toronto to Los Angeles, Italy to the UK, banging on pots and pans at 7:30 every night to give thanks to health-care workers, yes, but also to let everyone else know we're still here. We may have been locked down, but we could connect with each other (and get off social media). Together, we made one big, loud, appreciative noise.

As Hewak drove across Delhi Street a month after that first lockdown began, she saw a line of signs as she passed Guelph General Hospital. "Thank you front-line workers!!" "Thank you front-line heroes." Or, simply, "We are in this together." Hewak wondered how long it would last, this overt togetherness, this support for those who had "essential" jobs. Sure enough, she said, the signs came down a few months later, "probably around the same time the pandemic pay was clawed back."

While we might like to think we're all in this together, the pandemic affected people differently, often in ways that corresponded to their economic means: their income, type of job, and whether they had any family wealth or savings they could draw on all played a part in the choices people were able to make about their health, education, and work.

Many of the rich, for example, flew off to their tropical homes and lakeside mansions; those who had access to them escaped to cabins and cottages in the woods or to beach houses; those who could afford to tried to book a bolthole anywhere they could.

For those who could afford it, or whose job supported it, the pandemic became a chance to live and work

abroad. Between July 2020 and April 2021 *Forbes* magazine alone had no less than three articles on how to work
remotely. Particularly eager to attract temporary resi-
dents were places that had relied on tourism prior to the
pandemic to drive their economies: The Bahamas, for
example, might issue a visa if you could prove self-em-
ployment or supply a letter from your employer.[2]
Barbados offered a welcome if you could prove an annual
income of at least US$50,000.[3] Estonia also rolled out the
pandemic welcome mat, launching a digital nomad visa[4]
that allowed foreigners to live in the country for a year.
Given that the cost of living is 30 percent less in Estonia
than it is in the States,[5] it was understandably attractive
to those who were able to make a go of it.

High-income families, as well as those with jobs in
tech, finance, insurance, and some cultural industries
(those in media, publishing, and other creative professions, barring any who needed live shows or rehearsal
space to make a living), were mostly able to work at
home,[6] while low-wage and non-unionized workers and
employees in service industries (restaurants, retail) faced
job loss or, if they were lucky,[7] continued in essential jobs,
putting themselves at risk doing the work the rest of us
needed. Some delivered groceries to people's doorsteps,
people who then wiped down their deliveries with disin-
fectant before bringing them into their homes.

Those with children had different challenges. Parents
who had jobs where they could work remotely tried to do
so with their kids struggling to attend class via a com-
puter screen, or make it through school holidays with no
activities such as day camps, and little to no child care
available. As difficult as this was, it was easier for those

who could afford an internet connection and additional computers for their kids; those of lesser economic means were often not so lucky.

Lower-wage workers and their families were often living in cramped apartments, without internet access or computers for everyone. Provincial and federal governments acted as quickly as possible to try to get them the resources they needed, providing Wi-Fi and devices so children could learn remotely and, in some cases, providing income support so parents who lost their jobs wouldn't be left destitute.[8] This did little to help, however. And often parents whose work was deemed essential and could not be done remotely had to leave older siblings to look after the younger ones, so that neither could focus on their remote studies: the long-term consequences of this have yet to be measured.

The differences between those who had adequate resources and those who didn't quickly become apparent. In Toronto, for instance, statistics showed recent immigrants and people with low incomes were being hospitalized at four times the rate of everyone else, with a death rate twice as high.[9]

Crowded apartments, having to use public transit, working conditions that left people exposed to the virus, and not being able to afford to call in sick if they were feeling ill all led to increased rates of Covid-19 for less privileged groups. Toronto infectious disease expert Dr Isaac Bogoch pointed to these social and economic inequalities as part of the problem,[10] as well as highlighting outbreaks in prisons, food processing plants, work camps, and shelters as other areas for concern. He tried to focus our attention on the places and people "that *often exist beyond the focus of political attention"* (emphasis mine). Infections were also spreading quickly among migrant workers.

"If there is a silver lining in this pandemic," Dr Bogoch said, "[it's that] this has highlighted some of the inequalities that we see and has highlighted many of the needs of marginalized populations." That "silver lining" is an invitation to talk about those inequalities and to try to do something about them. They were manifested in ways that measure economic class: income, housing, jobs, and educational opportunities.

The pandemic had an early and profound effect on work and job losses. One study[11] found that nearly half of the jobs lost in the Canadian labour market were in the bottom earnings quartile—which represented jobs in industries such as accommodation and food services, where workers were mostly younger, paid hourly, and weren't part of a union.

Racialized workers also experienced deep unemployment. In a Canadian survey conducted between November and December 2020, the lowest unemployment rate was experienced by white Canadians at 7.4 percent. Black and Indigenous Canadians experienced an unemployment rate of nearly double, 13 percent, while other racialized people faced an 11.5 percent unemployment rate.[12] Growing inequality has made recovery for the disadvantaged more difficult and more likely to result in long-term negative effects.

Most people will say they work hard. People with higher incomes will say they worked hard to get where they are—long hours to climb the corporate ladder or studying to get to university. People with lower incomes work hard too: people on the front lines, in low-wage jobs, the essential workers who have cared for us.

Yet, if we are all in this together, and if this work is indeed essential, why are the people we've deemed to be so essential in a position where they are being forced by the pandemic to work even harder while getting sicker? To work hard yet be unable to afford the resources to educate their kids? What makes the jobs they're doing any more or less valuable than those professions that allow people to work from home? Why has the system been set up in this way? These are the questions Lise, for one, would like answered.

If we treat our "heroes" as second-class citizens, then we have to reimagine what it means to be a hero. The pandemic has created an opportunity to begin discussing what class means, and what we mean when we talk about it, much of which is driven by the way we measure socio-economic class.

I grew up poor, but now, despite this initial disadvantage, have been fortunate enough to arrive in a place where I have an education, a home with a yard, and a job I've been able to do at home throughout the pandemic. I'm involved in the publishing community, in my day job as books editor at the *Toronto Star*, and I see first-hand whose stories are published, and often whose aren't.

Over the next six chapters, I'll consider what we mean when we talk about class, how ideas around privilege and fitting in affect the way we navigate and see the world and our place in it, whose voices help define the conversations we do have around class, and why it's important to encourage the telling of and listening to even the most difficult stories—a basic dignity we all deserve.

What Do We Mean When We Talk about Class?

IN SEPTEMBER 2021, I went to a cocktail party, a book launch, the first since the Covid-19 lockdown began in March 2020. It was held outdoors at the Women's Art Association in Toronto. Founded in 1887 by women artists to support each other and to teach applied, fine, and performance arts, in response to the Arts and Letters Club's policy of limiting membership to men (the club didn't open its doors to women members until 1985), it was organized by people who understood what it was like to be left out of powerful organizations but who had enough power of their own to get something going for themselves.

It felt wonderful to be out amongst people again after months of lockdown. Small groups of people, some masked, some not, all double-vaxxed (befitting the latest protocol), formed, broke apart, and reformed, propelled by months of relative isolation, trying to get a feel once again for conversation and gossip and small talk. At one point, I found myself in a conversation that turned to back-to-school shopping. Talk meandered to school days and buying bags and backpacks and pencils and shoes and clothes. Against the backdrop of clinking glasses and trays of canapés, relaxing in the lovely gardens barely fifty feet from the busy and expensive Mink Mile shopping district along Bloor Street, the reminiscing contained both the warmth of nostalgia and the promise of new beginnings on an early September evening.

But reminiscing doesn't always mean the good old days, and new beginnings aren't promising for everyone. I couldn't share in the nostalgia, and, frankly, sometimes in conversations like these I want to shut it down—there's an assumption that everyone shares in it, and they don't. I don't recall ever having a backpack; I carried my books to school in a grocery bag. I sometimes got cheap pencil crayons; through all my years of schooling, I never had the Laurentians I really wanted as they were too expensive.

I remember, as a child, going to the mall at the beginning of school to get exactly one outfit, knowing that this and a few clothes at Christmas were all I was likely to get the entire year. The latest Jordache jeans? I could only dream. Friends would go to Jerry's to get discounted name-brand Lee and Levi's. I only ever went once, and the feeling that I, too, could buy what everyone else did was a treat; when I did shop, it was at the cheapest bargain stores. While the discussion of beloved brands and back-to-school shopping brought back fond memories for the group at the cocktail party, for me it triggered memories of what it was like to want. Of my schoolmates telling me that I smelled— my clothes hadn't been washed because there was either no change to feed the washing machines in the basement laundry room in our apartment building or because we'd run out of detergent and couldn't afford to buy any more.

We moved fourteen times during my childhood, often to small brick buildings, the sort you still see around town, gathered in clusters on main streets, tucked into residential neighbourhoods filled with post-war bungalows, near railroad tracks or strip malls, windows curtained with flags and tinfoil and old flowered sheets. During the pandemic, driving by these apartments, many without balconies, I'd think about the families inside; families with kids doing their best to keep body and soul and mind together. I had lived in those apartments myself as a child—the kind of apartment to which your parents move when they're poor, when there's little affordable or government subsidized housing; where the living areas were small, the television loud, and the bathroom the only place you might find a bit of privacy. With no balconies, they felt claustrophobic; to escape, we'd gather outside to play in the yard or hang out on the stairs leading into the building. With no elevators, tenants would haul their groceries up three flights of stairs, through halls smelling of fried onions and stale cigarette smoke.

While these examples might seem incidental, they give a glimpse of something larger, the simple things necessary to allow us to move through the world with dignity: A clear space to sit and do your homework. Clothes that fit, or that are at least clean. Soap and shampoo for self-care and basic hygiene. A home that feels safe and comfortable, the lack of which makes you feel like an outsider, like you don't belong; makes you feel *less than*.

And so, back at the cocktail party, I nodded, smiled,

but didn't say anything. I'm not quite sure why—this wasn't an unsafe crowd. Here I was now standing among them after all. The assumption of a shared experience told me something. I could talk about my experience as an adult—I'm middle-class enough now that I understood what they were talking about, the types of things I now regularly provide my own child.

Thinking back, I run through the reasons I didn't: the looks of pity I imagined I might get, stopping the conversation in its tracks, even if I made a joke about it. It's happened enough times before: Sharing my story with a former boss, only for her to say "*That* explains things." Explains *what*, exactly? Another saying, "Yeah, so what?"—indicating that they assumed my background, where one comes from, whether with advantages or not, doesn't matter, not understanding that it does. These are the times you roll your eyes and move away, hoping to find the other people in the room who also grew up poor—they're everywhere—and you can laugh and talk about the fabulous outfit you got at a thrift store, or how, by simple deep-frying, your cheap childhood dinner of mac and cheese suddenly becomes a fancy hors d'oeuvre, can you believe it? You might talk about how you managed to get to university, and how some people you know still buy Spam, not to be ironic, but because they like it.

Perhaps I was afraid they'd label me, that they'd realize—aha!—I was an imposter and didn't really belong. I might simply be so practised in not talking about things relating to class that I'm not sure how to begin a conversation about it. Maybe, in not sharing about myself, I lost an opportunity to begin a dialogue. Maybe there were other people there who felt the same way.

A few people left the group, and I decided to mention this project to those who remained. I could feel myself getting intense—I felt defensive, not sure how my opinions might land. "Class is the only -ism we don't talk about," said one person. "I've been thinking about it a lot lately," said another.

* * *

THE IDEA OF class first surfaced in the 1500s in Europe, but the term became more widespread during the late 1700s and 1800s. Class has been defined in terms of our relationships—to the land, or to the monarchy, the landed classes, the aristocracy.

In the mid-nineteenth century, German philosopher Karl Marx redefined classes in terms of their relationship to the means of production: landowners who made money from rent; the bourgeois (which included capitalists), who made their living from the profits of business; and the proletariat, who made their money by exchanging their labour for wages.[13]

Within those ideas of class were ideas of income, yes, but also of social standing and power. In France, the Bourbons ignored to their peril the desires of the commoners and peasants, and the French Revolution saw them dethroned and decapitated. The rise of the bourgeoisie saw the decline in power of the nobility—as their numbers swelled, the bourgeoisie agitated for change in the rules to benefit themselves, but they still needed someone to do the work.

Anglo-Dutch philosopher Bernard de Mandeville wrote in 1728 that "it would be easier, where property is well secured, to live without money than without the poor; for who would do the work?"[14] A few decades later, French philosopher Voltaire nodded to the same idea— "The comfort of the rich depends on an abundant supply of the poor"—although his focus was on human rights and equality.

Think back to the front-line workers at the beginning of the pandemic; they needed to keep working. As they served all of us, the gig economy, low wages, and precarious employment left them more vulnerable than most to Covid-19. The more things change . . .

* * *

WHEN WE DO talk about class today, we tend do so using the hierarchy of the upper class, the middle class, the working class, and the poor—and still assume that class defines a common set of interests or values.

The idea of the middle class is the one we hear about endlessly from politicians and mainstream media.[15] When trying to figure out what, exactly, we mean when we talk about class it makes sense to start here.

The Organization for Economic Cooperation and Development, in a 2019 report titled "Under Pressure: The Squeezed Middle Class,"[16] measures socio-economic class almost exclusively in terms of income.[17] The OECD looked at a range of countries, including Canada, to shed light on the group it calls "the main driver of economic growth and social stability."

It defines the middle class as anyone who earns between 75 and 200 percent of a country's median income (where half the population makes less than that amount, and half the population more). For Canada, the median income is $43,495 for a single person, so by the OECD's measure, the middle class in Canada includes any single person who makes between $32,621 and $86,990 a year—a range which incorporates more than 58 percent of the population. The lower-income class includes a single person who earns less than $32,621 (which in Canada accounts for 32 percent of the population); and the upper-income class is made up of the 10 percent of people who make more than $86,990 per year. While the fact that the middle class constitutes 58 percent of the population might at first glance sound substantial, context is important: measured against previous generations, there has been a steady decrease in the number of people who belong to the middle class: baby boomers had a 68 percent chance of being in the middle class, Generation X's chances decreased to 64 percent, and millennials' chances decreased to 60 percent,[18] a clear downward trend.

This broad-stroke approach has its limitations. For example, it doesn't take into account regional variations—in a country as big as Canada, there are stark differences in the cost of transportation, food, or housing in, say, Toronto, Ontario, versus Portage la Prairie, Manitoba, or Lunenburg, Nova Scotia. But it does provide us with an initial basis, grounded in hard data, to begin a conversation.

The OECD report goes on to offer up a number of remedies to combat the decline of the middle class, remedies familiar to anyone who has listened to political promises: decreasing taxes on "earnings" and hiking taxes on "capital and large inheritances"; building more affordable housing and helping "young people accumulate wealth"; modernizing "vocational education and training" and encouraging adult learning to improve skills, particularly digital skills.

While the OECD numbers spell out a specific income range, income doesn't tell the whole story about class. It doesn't answer how people feel about what their income buys them, or about what class they most identify with, or what their values are; it doesn't say whether members of a specific class feel any sense of well-being. Nor does it take into account the sense of identity that can unify people of similar economic and social backgrounds.

A 2017 survey by the Canadian polling firm EKOS[19] set out to examine how the decline of the middle class has affected feelings of populism, nativism, and racial intolerance. They asked a range of Canadians from all parts of the country and walks of life to self-identify as to which class they felt they were part of: poor, working class, middle class, upper class. Notably, EKOS did not define class in terms of specific income levels, nor did it provide any other indicator of what the categories might mean. It simply set out to measure how people saw themselves; how class *felt*. EKOS noted that, "at the beginning of the century, almost 70 per cent of Canadians located themselves in the middle class."

Not anymore. Now, the number is just 43 percent. The survey found that 13 percent of Canadians self-defined as poor, 37 percent as working class, 43 percent as middle class, and 4 percent as upper class. That's a drop of more than 25 percent in terms of those defining themselves as middle class over a brief seventeen years.

Similar to what was revealed by the OECD, the numbers of people who self-identified to EKOS as middle class were higher for older respondents, with 49 percent of baby boomers self-identifying as middle class, slipping to 45 percent for Gen X, 44 percent for millennials, and 39 percent for those under age thirty-five. Both reports indicate that fewer people from each generation identify as middle class.

While the EKOS survey included a working class category, another portion of the survey simply asked people whether, over the previous five years, they felt as if they were better or worse off financially, or had stayed about the same. The results were that 37 percent felt they had fallen behind, 38 percent felt as if they'd stayed the same, and 22 percent felt as if they'd moved ahead, meaning that 75 percent of respondents noted "either stagnation or decline."

The survey went on to break down respondents by whom they voted for, whether they or their parents were born in Canada, and whether they were university educated. Of university-educated respondents, 60 percent felt they were in the middle class, the highest amount, followed by 40 percent of college educated people, and just 28 percent of people who didn't graduate from high school.

In both the OECD and EKOS reports, the measure for seeing oneself as middle class is the belief in progress, that things will get better: that we will be better off than our parents, better off than we are today, that we will be able to move ahead, that we'll progress and prosper. But these surveys show something different: "The celebratory Bay Street outlook on the economy contrasts sharply with the unremittingly gloomy Main Street view," read the EKOS report.[20] Things weren't feeling like they should.

* * *

WHEN HE RAN for re-election in 2019, Prime Minister Justin Trudeau and his Liberal government unveiled an election campaign program titled "Real Change: A New Plan for a Strong Middle Class." It made promises to Canadians that sounded a lot like some of the OECD recommendations, including a new child tax benefit and income tax cuts. Economists and journalists crunched the numbers and found that the government's "middle class tax cuts" benefited people with higher incomes much more than people with lower incomes,[21] partly because the breadth of income was so wide, ranging from those making under $15,000 to those making $160,000. Even the OECD didn't define the middle class that broadly.

Trudeau's government also introduced a new high-level position: a minister of middle class prosperity. A newly elected Ottawa MP, Mona Fortier, was given the job and also named an associate finance minister. She came armed with an MBA and a background in communications and media and public relations.

When Fortier was asked by the CBC to define what the government meant by the middle class,[22] she didn't dwell so much on numbers in her response as she did on values: "I define the middle class where people feel that they can afford their way of life. They have quality of life. And they can ... send their kids to play hockey or even have different activities." She continued, "It's having the cost of living where you can do what you want with your family. So I think that it's really important that we look at, how do we make our lives more affordable now?"

Her answer was mocked by pundits across the country. If the government can't figure out what they mean by class, what value is there in their promises to an electoral "middle class"?

But Fortier had a point: the idea of being middle class

lies partly in *feeling* as if you're middle class. It's an identity intimately tied up with a set of values. As the authors of the EKOS report pointed out,[23] "The middle-class bargain was that hard work, innovation, and skill would yield a better future than one's parents and that your kids, in turn, would do better." Retirement security and the ability to afford a home were also part of that deal. This is the sentiment Prime Minister Justin Trudeau recognized with the use of the word prosperity. Belonging to the middle class is about having a certain way of life, or at the very least *feeling* that you have the possibility of attaining a certain way of life.

* * *

UNTIL A FEW decades ago, the graves of George Loveless and Thomas and John Standfield, men who came to Canada in the mid 1800s, drew little attention. Few, if any, realized their importance to the beginning of the modern labour movement. When John Clarke came to Canada from England in 1976, at the age of twenty-two, his initial stop was London, Ontario, where his father already lived. Shortly after Clarke arrived, his father made a unique discovery. "He wakes me up one morning," Clarke tells me, "and says, 'You'll never guess whose graves I found. But I'm not going to tell you—you're gonna have to come and see this. You won't believe it.'"

They walked a couple of miles down the road, Clarke recalls, before they were standing in front of several grave markers in Siloam Cemetery. Clarke recognized the names etched into the stone: they belonged to the Tolpuddle Martyrs. Clarke was gobsmacked. The group of six men were legendary in England; they'd helped to estab-lish what we now know as the trade union movement, which led to greater prosperity for workers for decades, even centuries, to come.

In 1834, more than thirty years before Marx published *Das Kapital* in Germany in 1867, six men from the village of Tolpuddle made the decision to start a trade union. Their decision came out of the Swing Rebellion (also known as the Swing Riots) of a few years earlier. New machinery and regulations were changing the rural way of life. Though the average family's weekly cost of living at the time was more than thirteen shillings, workers were only being paid a weekly wage of nine shillings. Workers rebelled, destroying threshing machines and setting fire to farms as they rioted and demanded better wages.

Many employers acquiesced and raised wages to stem the riots. Once order was restored, however, wages were once again cut.[24] Deciding there had to be a better way than violence, farm workers formed a union under the leadership of six men from the small village of Tolpuddle, in the county of Dorset—James Brine, James Hammett, George Loveless, George's brother James Loveless, George's brother-in-law Thomas Standfield, and Thomas's son John Standfield. All swore a secret oath to the newly established Friendly Society of Agricultural Labourers and agreed that they would not work for less than ten shillings a week, which though more than they were being paid, was by no means excessive: it was still three shillings under what we would today call a living wage.

While starting a trade union was legal, swearing a secret oath, it turned out, was not. A local landowner, James Frampton, found out about their secret pledge and led the charges against them. Like many landowners at the time, Frampton feared trade unionism would threaten the power base and wealth of the landed upper classes—he had witnessed the French Revolution and didn't want to see that history repeated in England.

"Make an example out of them," he ostensibly said—although some pointed out that what the Tolpuddle Martyrs were doing was no different than what the Orange Order had done, the difference of course being the Martyrs were labourers and the Orange Order included much of the establishment.

Nonetheless, the Tolpuddle men were sentenced to seven years' penal servitude in Australia. When they returned to England three years later, after being pardoned in 1837 as a result of strong public uproar, their experience had transformed them into martyrs and they became minor celebrities. Their notoriety, however, made it hard for them to gain employment. Eventually, five of them (all except Hammett) emigrated and settled near London, Ontario, and made a pact not to talk about their past so that they could build and live their lives in peace. John Standfield went on to become the mayor of his district.

They didn't want their history to be known so that it wouldn't affect their future. But it's a history, Clark says, that should be celebrated, that we should be proud of. Now, each May Day, there is a picnic in the park to commemorate their actions, actions which established the beginnings of the labour movement we know today.

The gravesites are about 120 kilometres to the west of Guelph, Ontario, where, almost two hundred years later, Lise Hewak and her fellow workers were caught up in similar circumstances: a shifting employment paradigm that attracted "hero" pay for a while, which then disappeared when employers no longer felt the pressure to pay it.

In 1990, fourteen years after his father's discovery, Clarke would found the Ontario Coalition Against Poverty, which promotes the interests of the poor and homeless, including advocacy for individuals dealing with government agencies such as the Ontario Disability Support Program, and fights to raise the minimum wage.

* * *

AS THE TRADE union movement matured, for which the Tolpuddle Martyrs helped pave the way, the landscape of aspiration changed. The union movement gave birth to what Toronto Metropolitan University sociologist Bryan Evans calls the "old left," encompassing communist and social democratic parties. They had a role in constructing class identity in both electoral and cultural terms.

In Evans's hometown of Sudbury, Ontario, for example, the International Union of Mine, Mill and Smelter Workers had a cultural director who would bring in the Winnipeg Ballet or offer cartoon mornings at the mine hall. The union also established a summer camp just outside the city, providing a place for union members' families to enjoy the beach, for children to attend summer camp and, as they aged, to become counsellors and gain leadership experience.[25] The union was doing more than bargaining—it was building a culture, providing a sense of belonging and of shared values.

"It was about constructing the sense of who you are as

an individual and the people within your life, where are you situated in the larger context of political and economic power," says Evans.

But things have changed. In 1981, when Statistics Canada started keeping track of such things, 38 percent of Canadian workers belonged to unions. In 2022, that number is just 29 percent.[26] Only about 14 percent of Canadian workers in the private sector now belong to a union[27]—a drop from 19 percent in 1997. In 2022, around 77 percent[28] of public service workers belonged to unions, an increase of a little over 11 percent from 1997.

If there's going to be a shared voice, it comes down to this question of organizing in workplaces, says Evans, no matter how much they might have changed from those early union years. "They may not be the mine and the mill anymore . . . it can be the office tower, the bank tower, the retail outlet, the Walmart, the Starbucks—the foundations of the service economy"—that part of the economy, he points out, which is highly polarized, encompassing everything from low-wage workers to those making incredibly high salaries "and everything in between."

It's not the case that no one in Canada, Evans notes, is talking about class and values. But it hasn't been a mainstream conversation "because there's nothing larger pushing these basic questions, these basic issues, in a very overt way onto the table."

* * *

ANOTHER THING THE Tolpuddle Martyrs symbolize: the idea of the so-called New World as a place where anybody can make it. They, like many immigrants to Canada and the United States before and since, chose to come to a place where they weren't dogged by their class or their actions and public reputation—where they felt they could make a better life for themselves. They were able to buy land (even if that land had only recently been taken from Indigenous peoples).

While the burgeoning union movement allowed more people to aspire to something better, so did the increased accessibility of education. Recognizing that the need to move to larger centres to access university education put such higher education out of reach for many people from regional communities, the government at the time established[29] universities in smaller, remote, or rural centres across the province. This also often resulted in, Bryan Evans points out when we speak, "the economic and social development of a region which had been relatively backward. There was value in that."

These investments proved very successful. The establishment of key regional universities changed the lives of subsequent generations of people and improved the economies of many parts of the province. In the 1980s, says Evans, various levels of government were subsidizing universities' costs to the tune of 80 percent. They understood that these investments were central to making Canada a more economically competitive country and to raising the standard of living for all citizens. These days, he says, it's more like 38 percent, although the Ontario Confederation of University Faculty Associations put government support of post-secondary education at just 24 percent in 2019.[30] As government subsidies have declined, universities have had to increase the cost of a university education for students. As a result, post-secondary education, particularly at the university level, is once again becoming inaccessible, with many young people either foregoing it entirely or being forced into so much debt that it will take them half a lifetime to pay off.

* * *

MILES CORAK IS an economist who specializes in income inequality, equality of opportunity, and intergenerational mobility. He is currently at the City University of New York, but he grew up in Canada, the son of Eastern European immigrants. He was the first of his cousins to be born in this country and was the only one to have been taught his parents' native language at home. Like most immigrants, he didn't have a wide network of connections that might provide easier access to jobs; he did not have the "soft skills" of engaging with people, nor did he have family money to fall back on or a family business to provide a job.

What he did have, he says, was an education that was paid for.

As he went through public school, in the late 1970s and early 1980s, and then on to community college, university, and graduate school, his education was funded by various government programs and scholarships. At the time, he says, "the Ontario government was giving people with my family background money. 'Here's your cheque, go to school.'"

And so he did.

That almost entirely funded education provided some of what the EKOS report highlighted as essential to feeling as if one belongs to the middle class: this government investment made Corak feel as if he belonged to the larger community while providing him a sense of motivation and hope for the future, an ability and opportunity to both imagine and aspire to something better. One of the most important things that access to educational opportunity provides is hope.

Education is also one of the factors the OECD[31] cites as a key to social mobility. In a foreword to its 2018 report *A Broken Social Elevator?*, OECD chief of staff Gabriela Ramos observes, "We have long emphasised the multi-dimensional nature of inequality. Socio-economic status heavily influences employment prospects, job quality, health outcomes, education, and the other opportunities (including access to relevant networks) that matter to people's well-being." In terms of education, Ramos notes, "Children whose parents did not complete secondary school have only a 15% chance of making it to university compared to a 60% chance for their peers with at least one parent who achieved [university or college-level] education."[32]

For Corak, the fully funded education to which he had access gave him the opportunity to pursue "a career path in which merit is clearly measured and demonstrated." As he put it, "you can't argue with transcripts, right?" With good grades and research skills, where he came from, what he looked and sounded like, mattered less. People didn't have to see him or interact with him personally to read and value his research, the success of which could be easily graded on merit.

"I study mobility because I've moved from being raised in a family in the bottom 5 percent, to raising a family in the top 5 percent," he said. "That's a background that's going to give me empathy and a perspective, and it influenced which branch of economics I went into."

One of Corak's studies measured the difference in mobility between the US and Canada.[33] It showed that there is a certain degree of mobility within the middle classes, or the range of middle-income earners, in both countries. But in the bottom 10 percent and the top 10 percent of income earners, there tends to be what he calls a stickiness—something he's studied in various ways, for example, by comparing intergenerational mobility in the United States versus Canada, and within the various regions of Canada.

The OECD has also recognized this difficulty of moving up from the bottom rungs or down from the top rungs of the ladder, labelling it as a "sticky floor" and a "sticky ceiling"[34] in its *Broken Social Elevator?* report, in which the authors note that "mobility prospects are not equally shared throughout the income ladder." Over a four-year period, it was found that "about 60% of people remain stuck at the bottom 20% of the income distribution." The stickiness at the top, it noted, was even "more persistent—70% remain there for four years. And those at the top are much more likely to remain there for their whole life: in the U.S. and Germany, almost half of the sons of rich fathers are in the top earnings quartile themselves."[35]

If there's a stickiness in the top and bottom, the middle offers the most income mobility. Sometimes this can mean opportunities, but it can also mean a deep and quick slide down the economic ladder as a result of unexpected events such as unemployment or divorce. Studies showed that "one in seven of all middle class households, and one in five of those living closer to lower incomes, slide into the bottom 20% over a four-year period," the OECD report notes.[36] It noted additionally that a further divide among the middle classes appeared in several countries: "for those closer to lower incomes and part of the 'bottom 40%', the risk to further slide down over the life course has increased."

That churn, particularly for the bottom 40 percent, results in insecurity. There's the idea, contrary to the middle-class agreement EKOS referred to, that even by working hard and playing by the rules, people feel resigned, that there's not much they can do to guarantee their children a better lifestyle than they've had: "It's the luck of the draw."

And increasingly that luck of the draw—the wealth of the family you were born into, job stability, where you live—seems more important than ever. As Evans pointed out, university students increasingly fund more and more of their own education. Economic growth helped provide much of the security and employment stability that Corak mentions. But many other factors can affect your luck: Economic turmoil—if you don't have the "right" job or the "right" investments, you can move down the economic ladder. A job that doesn't provide health benefits might ruin your family for a generation. Even those who own their own homes or have a decent income can drop social and economic classes if they're not lucky, even with an education. Even drawing the lucky straw of when and where you were born—in Canada, during the prosperous twentieth century, for example—might not be enough to ensure a sense of well-being.

* * *

BRYAN EVANS SUMS up the effect of all the caveats and confusions surrounding class, saying, "There are too many footnotes to make these popular conversations."

John Clarke feels that the ways we currently define class groups, particularly the middle class, are not useful. "This sort of notion of the amorphous middle class, it's a convenient thing. It is, first of all, a way of shaming the poorest working-class people; it's a way of creating this sort of sense of a rather snobbish place for people who do feel they have a right to claim themselves as the middle class; and it's a way of containing the envy for the people at the top. But I just don't think it corresponds to reality," he says.

"I'm less concerned about the debate about what the middle class is," Corak says. "Think of it as the broad majority of Canadians, period . . . But it stops you from doing more. It has built into itself a notion of deserving versus non-deserving, of merit-based supports . . . What if I don't work hard or can't work hard to join them? And why is that lifestyle more preferable than another lifestyle?"

But by not talking about class, we reinforce a narrative that is part of the very DNA of Canada and the United States, the narrative that anyone can achieve the American dream or its Canadian cousin, the opportunities are there for the taking. That if you work hard and pull yourself up by your bootstraps and follow the rules, you, too, may find yourself in a room with billionaires, and not on the outside looking in with the people who are just scraping by. The flip side of this egalitarian ideal is that if you don't make it, it's your own fault. So, if the dream is indeed going to be attainable, we have to talk about what it's going to take us to get there.

On Privilege and Expectations

THERE'S AN EVENT that takes place every year where wealthy revelers pay to attend a dinner to support the arts. There might be, say, forty tables, each with ten people at them, sponsored by banks, corporations, and various media outlets. An artist is featured at each table, feted as the honoured guest, sure, but also there to sing for their supper, to entertain and edify the donors who are paying the big bucks for their seat.

A couple of years ago, before the pandemic, dozens of artists milled with the media, corporate sponsors, politicians, and other dignitaries. The artists ate oysters from the bespoke oyster bar, sipped Moët, and generally enjoyed being amongst a crowd they wouldn't normally move in. At the tables during dinner, there was a silent auction. Bids, and the names of those doing the bidding, scrolled across a screen so that the other wealthy attendees would know when they'd been outbid, but it also served to show everyone at the gala who exactly was ponying up. There were some famous names, faces recognizable from the media for their business or cultural credentials. There were some old money families in the crowd, along with the newly rich, including people who had immigrated to the country and had quite clearly made it. And there was a certain amount of one-upmanship in the bidding. One person wrote a cheque for a few tens of thousands. The wife of a captain of industry was there with diamond and emerald chandelier earrings. "Are they real?" my seatmate and I asked each other. They had to be. She was known for her jewellery and her clothes; certain fashion reporters would later include her name in bold type along with that of the designer whose outfit she was wearing.

For the event, I'd hauled out a dress I recently bought at a local department store. Roaming the aisles, I saw one for $7,000—a beautiful designer dress made with velvet and lace, gorgeous jewel colours, a rich bohemian look. Out of my reach, but probably still too low-end for the woman with the chandelier earrings. I was happy enough with the dress I ended up with, black, neutral, bought for $120 on sale.

We were drinking the same champagne and noshing on the same food, but there were multiple parties going on in that room. For the philanthropists it was a social event, a chance to put one's money on display with designer clothes and jewels, say hello to other business and cultural leaders, or pony up a sizable cheque; for the artists it was a way of representing their community (as well as having a fun night out); for those at other corporate tables it was a party to which they were lucky enough to be invited.

I'm not sure which of the people in that room pulled themselves up by their bootstraps, who inherited family wealth, who in the crowd was lucky enough to have the connections, money, opportunities, expectations that allowed them to get to the upper echelons, and which of them felt entitled to be there. Did everyone understand their luck? Or did they assume that they deserved everything that came their way? Did they see themselves as self-made even if they'd had parental or family help? Or did they thank their lucky stars they had landed a good job?

That party is a good metaphor for the way class works, particularly in modern cities. We live cheek by jowl, we share facilities. The place where this event was held is usually open to the public and often provides a spot for people who are homeless or lonely to spend the afternoon or evening; it was closed for the party to raise funds for the facility's ongoing activities. Some of those homeless people hung around outside, having no where else to go. At the end of the night, chauffeured limousines or Cadillac Escalades came for the rich; taxis or Ubers for those with a bit of money or whose employers provided expense accounts or taxi chits; others drew coats over their fancy frocks and headed to the subway.

The people sitting outside would be there in the morning when the doors opened to the public once again.

* * *

EACH PERSON IN that room was privileged. What do I mean by that? According to the Oxford English Dictionary the word simply indicates "a special right or advantage that a particular group or person has." Privilege itself isn't a negative word: it becomes that when it's weaponized, when it becomes personal, or when it goes unacknowledged.

The people in that room—we; I was there too—had many special advantages: we were at an exclusive event, organized by those who had the influence to close public doors for a private function that others couldn't get into; we were served oysters and champagne, food unaffordable to many people. Yes, everyone was there to support a good cause—the money raised would go to programs to support numeracy and literacy initiatives, create after-school programs, afford access to computers and online information—worthy and necessary programs and services for those who wouldn't otherwise have access to them because of lack of money, a stable home, or other reasons. But attendees were privileged as well in their ability to donate *more* money and exercising the choice to do so through the silent auction or with an extra donation that would have a direct effect on how the people outside those doors were able to experience the facility once it re-opened.

You could say they were using their advantage, their privilege, to try to create access for others; you could also say they were able to choose which people with less advantage they would give funding to.

The ultimate privilege might be the ability to set your own salary. In August 2021, Rosa Saba, then a business reporter at the *Toronto Star*, tweeted: "Millions of working Canadians saw their incomes devastated by the pandemic—but thanks to millions in bonuses, Canada's top execs did just fine."[37] The accompanying article explored how Canadian corporations were "tweaking" the formulas used to determine bonuses so that CEOS didn't see a reduction in their incomes, even during the pandemic.[38]

These executives run the companies, so they have the power to set the rules in their favour, and they've been increasingly doing so. Consider these numbers: between 1978 and 2018, CEO compensation has grown 940 percent while worker compensation has grown only 12.[39] In 2021, typical CEOs in the United States earned 351 times what the typical worker did.[40] This growing disparity has led to a range of consequences that we all have to deal with, from political turmoil to increased poverty and homelessness, though few of the high rollers at the cultural gala seem to be worried about it.

Understanding how people got to be in that room matters: they are in a position to make choices that have an impact on those who don't have power. And they are in a position to make choices that reinforce their own status and power.

That's privilege: being part of a system that can be tweaked in your favour and having the power to do so. It's also the privilege of being able to give some of that money away in an act of philanthropy if you wish. But that act of philanthropy doesn't make up for stacking things increasingly in one's own favour, and if things were more equitable, perhaps institutions like the one hosting this gala wouldn't be so reliant on the generosity of a handful of donors.

Understanding the barriers to mobility—the things that prevent those in need of resources from moving into decision-making positions that help decide who gets those resources and how—is important to staunch growing inequality and the problems inequality results in.[41]

Growing inequality is leading to greater political division, and recent studies show that even those in privileged positions, those with more money and opportunity and greater expectations, are far less happy when inequality is left unchecked[42]—mainly because they're looking around to see how much others have and how they measure up. Nevertheless, it might not be possible to convince the lady with the chandelier earrings or the guy who wrote out the cheque for tens of thousands of dollars they'd be happier if things weren't quite so unequal.

* * *

CHELENE KNIGHT GREW up in Vancouver's Downtown Eastside. She led a nomadic childhood, living in twenty to thirty different places during the 1980s and 1990s. Her mother, who "struggled with addiction and sex work," moved around with Knight and her younger brother in tow. It's a childhood Knight documented in her 2018 memoir *Dear Current Occupant*, addressed to the people who now live in those places. As a child, Knight rarely had any warning before she was forced to flee one place for another and was often told to "pack what you can" before almost immediately moving to another temporary home, living sometimes in flats, at others in single rooms in shared apartments; sometimes squeezed in with her family, sometimes with her own space.

It was a long climb from those inauspicious beginnings to the bright, sunny office where she takes a Zoom call with me. Knight now owns a business, a creative studio working with writers. She is a literary agent. She's an author. To get here from there she worked three jobs, supporting herself through school. She still works a number of jobs, since these new ventures are still growing and don't yet necessarily pay all the bills.

Knight is, by any measure, a success: she's overcome obstacles, created a career, owns a home. But she doesn't always *feel* as if she's a success. She recalls a conversation with a close family friend who learned that not only did Knight own her own business, she had staff who worked for her. "He kind of cuts me off and says, wait a minute, *you* have people working under *you*? And he just couldn't go any further with the conversation unless I explained myself." He knew her background, how she had grown up. He knew her family, what opportunities were open to her and the limited expectations for her when she was younger. Because of this, she says, "he was unwilling to see beyond that."

It left her feeling as if she had to explain herself. It's exhausting, she says. You continue "to climb and climb and climb and are always pushed back down by that . . . feeling of, well, I have to be ready to explain this."

The disconnect between who she is and how she sees herself and how other people see her is apparent in other ways too. She owns a home with her partner; it's part of a new housing development. When Knight, who is mixed race, answered the door to a person from the community association, he seemed surprised to see her. "If my white, middle-aged husband had answered the door, would the reaction have been the same?"

She has worked hard for everything she has. She has earned her position, her business, through her own merit—by the grades she achieved, the risks she took, the self-discipline she exerted. She was not given a leg up financially; her family had no network or connections. But, even now, there's a lingering feeling of not-enoughness. She feels uncertain about whether she belongs or how far she can go. There's a feeling, she says of "having to prove something beyond what everyone else in the room has to do."

Sometimes at the beginning of a meeting, people will make small talk about where they went on vacation, or their weekend away, their cabins or cottages or country homes. Knight understands that these types of conversations are important to building a congenial business relationship, but she finds that, often, she is worried about the fact that this small talk is taking up time—and, because she has to move on to the next job of the day, she feels less able to afford to spend her time with this sort of chat.

"If I have one task in front of me and all of my other needs are met by someone else, whether that's a partner or having some inheritance money or some kind of cushion so I don't have to worry about doing added projects, what does the hard work look like then? When you've got nothing else distracting from this task?" Knight asks.

Definitions become important: What does "hard work" mean? Hard work will mean something different to a person whose family owns a business and is able to give them a job than it will to a person who had no parental support and had to work two jobs in order to put themself through school. Sometimes, starting a conversation requires a backward glance: if someone thinks they have worked hard, it's worth unpacking what that means for them. What were they able to focus on—school? volunteer work? unpaid internships?—that enabled them to get to that point in their careers?

"I think the reasons these conversations are often ignored or swept under the rug is because they are uncomfortable," says Knight. "I also don't think we have a way into these conversations. How do we begin to unravel such a complex web of things?"

* * *

THE DIMENSIONS OF Poverty Hub was developed by Statistics Canada—the agency responsible for gathering data on the country's population, resources, economy, society, and culture—to track a wide range of variables that inform what it calls "deep poverty." It defines people living in deep poverty as those individuals whose family disposable income is 25 percent below Canada's poverty line. In other words, these are the poorest of the poor.

The hub was developed in order to measure the effectiveness of various actions and investments made by the federal government as part of its "Opportunity for All" anti-poverty strategy. The goal is not only to lift people out of poverty, but also to help them join the middle class and stay in it once they get there. To measure how effectively various government initiatives are working and recognizing that fighting poverty needs a multi-dimensional approach, the hub created a dashboard to track progress by measuring twelve indicators across three categories: dignity; opportunity and inclusion; and resilience and security.

Dignity is about stabilizing people and getting them out of deep poverty by ensuring that their basic needs, such as access to affordable housing, healthy food, and health care, are met. Within this category, indicators measured include how many people are living in deep income poverty, how many people are experiencing food or housing insecurity, and how many have unmet health-care needs.

While dignity is about stabilizing people, *opportunity and inclusion* aims to help people join the middle class (defined by median income) "by promoting full participation in society and equality of opportunity." Progress is tracked year to year by measuring indicators such as how many people are in the bottom 40 percent of income; how many Canadian youth (ages fifteen through twenty-four) are employed, seeking education or training; and how many Canadians have low literacy and numeracy skills.

Once people are lifted out of poverty and into the middle class (again, as defined by median income), *resilience and security* becomes the concern. The goal is to protect "Canadians from falling into poverty by supporting income security and resilience." The indicators tracked include median hourly wage, the poverty gap (how many people live below Canada's poverty line), and how many people have enough savings to cover three months' expenses in case of emergency (at the low income measure).[43]

These indicators are measured from year to year, charting how policy changes, economic conditions, and other variables are having an impact. So, for example, food insecurity (one of the measures that falls in the category of dignity), was a moderate or severe factor for 10.8 percent of all people in 2019, rising to 11.2 percent in 2020, perhaps reflecting the effects of Covid-19.[44]

* * *

THE WISTERIA VINES meandering around her central Toronto backyard are an interesting contrast to the large tobacco leaves Teresa Toten picked to earn money when she was eleven years old. We are sitting in her garden in mid-July—the showy, confident flowers are gone for the season, but the fecundity of the vines wrapped around an archway speak of the promise of next year. The Governor General's Award–winning writer of young adult books, including *The Unlikely Hero of Room 13B* and *Eight Days*, sits comfortably with a beer, the faint hum of cars punctuates the background of our conversation.

It's a far cry from the way Toten began life in this country: her parents fled Zagreb, Croatia, in 1955 when she was a day old; her mother came from a family of landowners who refused to embrace the communist regime, her father was a Canadian who was able to get them into this country and away from the dangers of a dictatorship.

When Toten was just seven months old, her father died, and her mother struggled financially after that. As a child, Toten was mostly left on her own and, as she describes it, she often "got into a great deal of trouble." It was the kind of trouble that didn't come from maliciousness but from not knowing how to take care of herself. Childcare was expensive, and Toten was often left to fend almost entirely for herself as her mother worked multiple jobs to support them. Once, Toten recalls, she'd emptied a can of cream of mushroom soup into a pot and put it on the burner— nobody had told her she had to add milk. "That burns really nicely," she recalled. She and her mother had lived in a flat in a house at the time, and the landlady didn't appreciate the smoke and burning smell. They were asked to leave. In another flat, she pretended to be Tarzan in the kitchen, swinging from cupboard to cupboard on an imaginary vine. The cupboards all came down.

She got her Social Insurance Number when she was eleven so she could work in the tobacco fields, manual labour which paid well compared to other jobs and even offered upward mobility for some farm workers.[45] "Tobacco was good money . . . for good reason," Toten said. "[The work] was dirty and hard." While the idea of what makes for "good money" is relative, Ontario had only recently, in the mid-1960s, implemented a mandatory minimum wage—with men to earn at least a dollar an hour and women eighty-five cents, although this didn't apply to agricultural workers.[46] By comparison, during the tobacco harvest in 1959, a few years before the province-wide minimum wage was implemented, daily wages for adult men working in those fields was thirteen dollars a day[47], a substantial premium over even the minimum wage five years later.

In Toten's leafy backyard that warm summer's evening, a plate of cheese and a glass of wine and a beer on the table in front of us as we chat, we're not far from the high school where her vice-principal recognized her academic ability and sat her down and helped her fill out university and scholarship applications, including to Columbia University and Trinity College at the University of Toronto. She had no idea how to do that, she says, and considers herself lucky to have had teachers who encouraged her, guided her—showed her what was possible, believed she was capable of doing it, and helped her find a way. Role models and mentors are important: parents might want the best for you, but they don't always know how to get there themselves, much less show their children the way.

She went on to U of T's Trinity College because her teachers pushed her toward it; she won a bursary and studied political economy. Those few affirmative statements are the shorthand of a life: what one doesn't see is the struggle and uncertainty. When she got to university, she says, she saw her schedule, saw that she had two classes on Monday, and a few on other days, and thought she had all this time. "I started working full-time at the Sheraton Hotel, which had just opened up," she says. "I had no idea how to study, I never had to study in high school." She was getting Cs, was close to losing the bursary, and the administration let her know they were disappointed in her. "I was terrified, it was humiliating, I wanted to quit," she said. "Mama put her foot down: 'We're not quitters! You don't need the job. Quit the job.'" It was a very difficult thing for someone who had always needed to work so that she could contribute to her family to do. But she cut her hours at the hotel and learned how to study. She found it hard to make friends—not because the well-off students didn't want to be friends, she says, but because she felt uncomfortable. "They all had two or three houses and vacations in Europe and camp. There was nothing I could relate to."

Almost failing, not measuring up in social terms. "The shame dogged me." These uncertainties seemed to prove that she didn't belong there. She went through a period of thinking, "Who did I think I was?"

Now, as an alumnus who eventually graduated, Toten gives lectures to students at Trinity College, and she tells them this: "If you don't even know there's a door there, how can you go through it? [If you're] of a certain class . . . you don't know where the door is. You don't even know there is a door. You really are dependent on well-meaning teachers, maybe neighbours, a coach . . . who sees there can be more."

That's if you're lucky. Not everyone has teachers who care.

There are assumptions made around students based on socio-economic circumstances and based on race about which, Toten notes, we're much more aware than we ever used to be. "Every BIPOC kid who is assumed to be not worthy of full attention; every East Asian kid assumed to be going to university . . . There's an immediate presumption by teachers and everyone around you. 'This kid doesn't have a chance.' Or 'This kid's going places.' They could be getting the same marks, parents working hard, six days a week, all of that. And one kid will be hustled along, and the other kid will be ignored and assumed to be a troublemaker."[48]

* * *

ANY TIME A person is chosen over another for reasons that aren't obvious is an example of privilege at work. How can you hope to follow unspoken rules? What does that teach a child about the idea of merit? How does one person get the extra boost where another doesn't? Why should one child's future be so precarious, while another gets a leg up in a different direction? We hear, and wish to believe, that society is a meritocracy; but if it were a meritocracy, every smart kid who wanted to go on to have some form of post-secondary education would be able to go; everybody could find a way to the job they want and deserve, even without family connections.

If our society were a meritocracy, the rules for progressing would be set out, or at least easy to discern. It makes those of us who grew up unaware of the rules second guess ourselves, even as adults; it makes those of us who were privileged enough to fit into the system's norms assume we are there because we deserved to be.

Toten notes that, today, the ability to get a toehold in the professions is even more difficult for those without money than it was when she was starting out. "The propensity toward internships leaves people who need to work to put themselves through school at a disadvantage. It's not enough to graduate with a degree; you need to approach with a resumé"

And often it's only the most privileged who are able to do that—students who don't need to support themselves or contribute to their family finances. Key findings by the Conference Board of Canada in a March 2022 report found that internships, or "experiential learning," don't always provide a level playing field. "Unpaid internships present a barrier to students from low-income families and . . . are often a barrier for all but the most privileged students."[49]

Toten's story speaks to her own grit and resilience; it also speaks to the lengths to which her mother went to provide for her child and make a better life for them both. Work hard, do whatever you need to succeed. These are the kinds of qualities politicians and social agencies often encourage when issues of class are raised, as if they believe that the only thing separating those making minimum wage from their middle-class "betters" is a lack of hard work and grit.

* * *

IF SOMEONE ASKED me when I was growing up what I wanted to be, I wouldn't have put secretary on the list. I saw myself as more of a career person, like the ones in books I read, but at fourteen, when I was choosing my high school courses for grade ten, I was keenly aware of one thing: I needed to make sure that I had the skills to get a good job. My parents split up when I was eight years old, dividing us into two single-parent households. I lived full-time with my mother; my father had visitation rights. When I was between the ages of eight and fourteen my mother moved with my brother and me seven times—my high school would be the eleventh school I'd attended—and money was always tight. There were no extra funds for karate lessons or summer camp; I babysat my younger brother in the summer once I turned twelve to save on childcare costs.

All of the issues I faced—housing instability, lack of access to education or extracurricular activities, expensive childcare—are still with us, as the Dimensions of Poverty Hub indicates. My experience from the 1970s and 1980s is being repeated today—headlines still regularly highlight the lack of affordable housing, the waiting lists for kids' activities, the high cost of education, expensive childcare. We haven't come that far.

I knew that, once I graduated from high school, I would need to take care of myself. So, I chose courses that would make me immediately employable: typing, shorthand, dictaphone/transcription. Secretarial skills. Skills that, ironically, would later stand me in good stead as a journalist. But this level-headed practicality had consequences that I couldn't have foreseen when I made the decision.

At the time, there were two levels of high school diploma you could achieve in Ontario: with the first you graduated grade twelve, after which you could get a job or go to community college, but university was closed off to you. The second option required a fifth year of high school, for which you earned an "honours" graduation diploma, which was necessary to go on to university. Only those who took courses in the academic stream could go on to grade thirteen. As this was considered "extra," students who chose to do so had to buy their own textbooks.[50]

And so, for the courses beyond the secretarial, I chose courses in the academic stream, so that the doors to a university education might someday be open to me.

But by the second semester of grade thirteen, I couldn't afford to buy those books. My parents were always complaining about money. I was eighteen years old, had a high school diploma, and figured maybe it was time to go out and earn a living, to help out—a classic working-class stance. I started looking in the want ads for a full-time job and quickly landed one at an import-export association. It paid minimum wage but came with a prestigious title: secretary to the vice-president. I went to the guidance office at school and dropped out. No one tried to dissuade me. No one talked to me about my future. No one asked me about my aspirations. I am still surprised no one offered any kind of support. Maybe my choices, fueled as they were by poverty and insecurity, had already locked in my future: by choosing skills-based courses that would make me employable, I had created a perception that that was all I aspired to. Maybe my teachers just assumed that my having a job, any job, was good enough.

I was fired within three months after botching a complex courier mailing. "Oh don't worry," said the chipper Kelly Girl recruitment lady at the employment agency. "I got fired from my first job too. We'll find you another." I soon began working as a temp at a sales office for business paper products, filling in for the full-time admin assistant. "Another day, another $1.50," she said on payday. "I got a raise," she explained. She looked at her credit card bill. "That's all you get this month." On the one hand, I admired her: an independent, working woman able to buy her own stuff, credit card bills notwithstanding. On the other hand, I thought: "Is that all there is?"

I was lucky: I had glimpsed a future I didn't want. More importantly, I now had the money for those textbooks. I quit the job and went back to high school to finish grade thirteen, having missed a semester. I gained the nickname "dropout"—which, though said laughingly, still hurt. I hadn't told anyone why I'd left school—the shame of not having enough money kept me quiet. I enrolled in Accounting and Economics and English and History and German, trying to create a different path forward.

As the end of high school approached, everyone around me was making plans. The parents of most of my schoolmates hadn't gone to university themselves—they were "new" Canadians, had come here to give their kids a chance at a better life, and most of my friends were expected to attend university. There was emphasis on study above all else.

I hadn't been a particularly good student. I had missed out on key concepts by moving from school to school; adapting to new teachers, new ways of doing things, making new friends. At home—I was now living with my father because of abuse from my mother's boyfriend—there was nowhere to do homework. My bed was a sofa in the living room. I could never save money from my part-time job—

although both my parents worked, their working-class jobs didn't pay enough to support a household on their own, and they often called on me to help pay bills, even to buy groceries. Once, when my father's girlfriend couldn't pay her gas bill, I did. Those were the values I was brought up with: you helped each other out. You were "good people"— the moral code of the working class: People might fall down, might struggle, might have demons or mental illness. But good people help each other out. "He'd give you his last dime," is the ultimate compliment. Even if you could use that last dime yourself, sometimes you give that dime away anyway and hope there'll be someone around to give you theirs if you ever need it.

Better yet, you hope you never need it.

* * *

"I DON'T KNOW if you can transcend class," says Kiké Roach. "You're born into the family you're born into." We're talking by phone, mid-pandemic, about class, her own work as a lawyer, and her parents who, while they both grew up in Trinidad, grew up in vastly different class situations.

Her father, Charles Roach, a lawyer and anti-poverty activist, was born in Trinidad. His father, Kiké says, was a trade unionist who worked in the oil fields of Trinidad and "so was able to amass some material wealth." His family was ambitious and had ambitions for him. Her father, she says, was expected to "try to get some kind of leadership [role] or try to gain some level of importance, get a higher education. In fact, my grandmother converted the family from Anglicanism to Catholicism because she thought that was the best school."

But there was nowhere for him to go in Trinidad after high school as a result of the limited opportunities the entrenched island colonialism offered (the best jobs were reserved for white people), so he came with his brother to Canada. Black men from the Caribbean during the 1950s were only likely to get one of two jobs: as a porter on trains[51] or as serving staff of some sort. Her father and his brother, though, set their sights on university. "They looked for the cheapest place they could go," she says, and so ended up at the University of Saskatchewan.

Her father and uncle are, Roach says, the exception to the usual immigrant story. Most Caribbean immigrants at the time remained labourers, becoming welders or transportation or maintenance workers, "people working with their hands." Her father and uncle faced barriers to mobility when they moved here in the 1950s, and, she says, people from the Caribbean are still facing barriers to mobility in Canada today.

"Even now, every single year Canada is importing Caribbean, migrant workers to grow our food and pick our crops and sending them right back," she says. "They're not able to gain Canadian citizenship because the temporary foreign worker program prohibits them from doing that. So there [are] . . . structural bars to class mobility, and a lot of the time they're not even questioned."[52]

Roach's mother, who also grew up in Trinidad, was born into a much different class experience than her husband, in what Roach calls a "hard-to-describe" class background. Roach's grandmother was the product of an illicit affair between her great-grandmother, a white Portuguese woman, and a Black Francophone man; her mother kept her, but she "was basically treated like a domestic by her

own mother." Roach's grandmother learned to be resource-
ful and went on to raise her own family of eight children
mostly on her own ("my grandfather was a tailor and wasn't
good with money at all"): she took in washing, took in
boarders, and ended up, at one point, owning three homes.
All of her children graduated at least from high school,
including Roach's mother, who was kept on to teach
younger students. "At nineteen she was basically a teacher
herself." But the only way for her to access post-secondary
education was to win an island scholarship. She didn't, and
she wasn't able to go to university. "She didn't have the
financial means."

The fact that her mother grew up in a class where she
wasn't able to go to university, while Roach's father was
expected to acquire a leadership role of some kind, was
one mark of the class difference between her parents,
Roach says, that "stayed with them all their lives." Her
father, she said, could have followed a path that would
have made him much wealthier than he became, but he
made certain decisions about how he was going to prac-
tice law that "left us clearly not in the upper-class bracket,
but the middle-class bracket." He and her mother, who
together ran the law office they founded, with her mother
as the office manager, made a conscious choice to represent working-class or poor people.

Roach spent her own life growing up as "in-between."
She lived in between a rich area and a poor area—in "a
grand old Victorian home with a winding staircase that
was built in the 1800s and was probably at one point
owned by a captain of industry" but that, in the 1980s,
was run-down, a project her parents hoped to renovate
one day. It was a time when sex workers walked the

streets near their home. She had never thought about being rich or poor. Although she is now, she says, fully aware that "I went to McGill University and studied law, I went on exchange and I lived in France for a year . . . I was called to the bar . . . and now I'm teaching as a professor [at Toronto Metropolitan University]. That, she says, is the trajectory of someone who could be considered as having quite a privileged life.

She became a lawyer like her father. "We were raised by activist parents, so it was really instilled in us from a very young age that social justice is what you're supposed to be pursuing." She went on to work at the same law office her parents founded, taking on the same kinds of clients and cases.

At times she's been criticized for that, being told "how dare you talk about racism and sexism and inequality . . . look at the life you've lived." Anytime there is a critique of the system, she says, there will always be people who will say Canada is a great country that offers opportunity to immigrants. "There's no doubt that that's true. But not everybody has the same experience."

Her parents, she says, felt it was important at demonstrations to get people to speak for themselves. And rally people to listen to those stories. They wanted those in power to pay attention to the ways that people's opportunities or human rights are trampled on.

Those are stories we still need to hear today.

* * *

THE IMPORTANCE OF seeing yourself reflected in your community and of knowing that it supports you, that it's there for you can't be overstated: it shapes your expectations and allows you to see different possibilities.

I was always told I could be whatever I wanted to be, but my family didn't know how to get there, exactly. My father hadn't finished high school. My mother had taken a few evening courses in university. No one else on either side of my family had gone on to post-secondary education, talent and intelligence notwithstanding. When I looked in the mirror, I was conflicted. On the one hand, I aspired to be like the girls I read about in books, or like Mary Tyler Moore—independent, career-oriented. On the other hand, I didn't see a person who could climb her way out of our one-bedroom apartment and into a college dorm. I didn't think I belonged on the bottom rungs of the socio-economic ladder, but I didn't know how to get myself much higher either.

I went to the guidance counsellor. She looked at my best marks: the secretarial courses and English.

"You could be a court reporter," she suggested. She didn't once mention going to university.

* * *

THE WORKING POOR, or those who grew up that way, talk about working hard from an early age, or valuing "good people," or not putting on "airs and graces." There is a down-to-earth stoicism that gives dignity to the idea of being poor, romanticizing it and making it seem acceptable, if not quite enviable.

But in "modern poverty," Jeremy Seabrook writes in *The Guardian*, "it seems the poor have internalised the assessment of—who? Their betters, the rich, legislators, moralists?—and are ready to accept responsibility for what has, through the ages, been seen as a visitation by chance, fate, even God, but not necessarily, at least until the industrial era, evidence of their own failings."[53] In other words, poverty, wealth, and class were historically viewed as having more to do with luck or fate (where you were born, when you were born, and to whom you were born) rather than being a direct result of one's own actions.

What do we mean by luck? The dictionary definitions simply point to "the force that causes things, especially good things, to happen to you by chance and not as a result of your own efforts or abilities" or "success achieved by chance."

As with privilege, it becomes a problem when it's weaponized or goes unacknowledged. We all have bigger or smaller bits of luck that affect us: the luck of being born in a country that's not mired in war or in the twenty-first century with modern medical advances; the luck of weather patterns that haven't left those of us who live in Canada in drought; the luck of being born to certain parents with a certain skin colour in a certain class; the luck of having a teacher that recognized your potential and asked you to participate.

The idea of luck comes with its own issues—that the spot you're in is one you can't get out of no matter how hard you work; or that those born into power or in the upper classes "deserve" to be there because it's fated. Or even that it's not to be questioned too much.

Seabrook argues that the idea that poverty is somehow connected to a person's own decisions or failings is relatively new. Poor people have traditionally shown "solidarity, even defiance, facing the condition of being poor. Why should shame be the particular inflection of poverty in this enlightened age?"

Because, he writes, that's how people in power spin it. How else do you explain voters of all classes voting in Conservative governments which cut social programs? When those in need of such programs are portrayed as somehow being at fault for their own poverty, cuts to social programs become easier to sell.

And if you're poor and you internalize that shame, your circumstances become something you don't want to talk about. You walk into a room and don't feel as if you belong. Or perhaps you figure that your situation is nobody else's business. But when this happens, we don't share our stories, which means that those whose experiences and backgrounds are different than our own never really come to understand our day-to-day life and what it might take to transcend the challenges we face, challenges that they've perhaps never thought of, let alone experienced. And then those with the power to make the changes that could lead to more equality and everyday dignity don't understand the urgency, and the same policy decisions keep being made and the gap between the poor and the rich continues to widen.

The idea of "betters" implies a value judgment—that those who have material wealth are intrinsically worth more in their humanity, and those who have less material wealth are somehow less hardworking or less valuable.

"Shame is about the most useless emotion you can have," Toten says. "Shame gives you nothing. It teaches you nothing. It pins you down and holds you there... I've seen it happen too many times."

*   *   *

WHEN I WAS in grade eight, we were evicted from our subsidized apartment in one of the poorer areas of Toronto. I was a kid, I don't know the reasons and straight answers can be hard to come by. What I do know is that I came home from school to find a yellow sheet of paper from the Sherriff's office taped to the door and that my key wouldn't fit in the lock. I sat down in the hallway, crying, wondering what to do.

Kind neighbours took me in as I tried to get hold of my mother to tell her what had happened. Within a few days our possessions were thrown into boxes, tossed into the back of our ancient blue Rambler or left behind. We moved to a much smaller apartment at the other end of the city, and I started at yet another school. When the possibility of subsidized housing doesn't exist for those in crisis, the choices for affordable living are limited.

The new apartment was dark and damp. Where, a few weeks before, we would have taken an elevator up to a carpeted hallway, and the only steps were down to the sunken living room, now we took old tiled stairs down to a dark, echoey basement hallway, our apartment only a few doors from the rattle of the laundry room's washers and dryers. In the kitchen, dirt gathered where the corners of the old linoleum had curled and broken. I looked out the bedroom window, my eyes level with the street. A chip in the paint showed layers of lives coloured in blue, white, pink, beige, yellow, and the muddy green that now covered the walls.

But the part of the city we moved to was nicer, with more single-family homes and leafy streets; the school I went to was better, too, with teachers who worked to include me in class and in extra-curricular activities, even though I started halfway through the school year. I joined the after-school choir, ran in the city cross-country meet, came amongst the top in my school on a standardized test, read aloud in class stories I'd written—and people liked them. One day, a friend introduced me to a boy who smelled of clean laundry. He asked me where I lived. I told him. "You live *there*?" he asked, surprised. He lived in one of the post-war bungalows that populated the rest of the area; the kind of home where, I imagined, he lived a life free from the drudgery and dirt and abuse and addiction and eccentric characters crowded into our little brown building. This was a small moment, but it's the sort of moment that helped me see other possibilities: even if he was surprised at where I lived, I could hold my own. Those little moments are the kind that help lift you up if you let them.

* * *

WHEN WE TALK about class, part of what we talk about is our expectations: of what type of education or job we might aspire to; of networks and connections—whether through family, friends, or work—that can help us; possibly of owning a home. All these factors help provide a safety net, a sense of comfort, knowledge that you have the skills you need, someone to help you out, or a cushion of equity in your home or investments if the going gets tough.

Canadians still overwhelmingly aspire to home ownership—according to a 2016 poll, 85 percent feel it is a priority.[54] But, as home prices have risen and it's become more difficult for young people to save for a down payment, the possibility of home ownership is now often dependent on parental help or an inheritance. In Ontario, 40 percent of parents of younger homeowners assisted their children financially, with the average gift being more than $70,000.[55]

"Boomers have been paying off their homes," the *Globe and Mail* reported in March 2021, "and now have a lot of money to play with. And give away."[56] They've also been on the receiving end of inheritances worth some $750 billion from their parents,[57] the so-called Silent or Depression Generation, born between 1928 and 1945, in what's been termed the "great wealth transfer." Coined by financial planners in the US and used by planners here in Canada, too, the phrase describes the inheritances that are continuing to accrue to the baby boom generation from their parents—and will continue for the next few decades as the boomers, those born between 1946 and 1964, transfer that money and more to succeeding generations—their Gen X and millennial kids and grandkids.

Think about it: while this wealth transfer affects close to 48 percent of the population, that means 52 percent of the population is *not* expecting an inheritance. There's no planning for a great wealth transfer when there is no wealth to transfer. The passing down of intergenerational wealth helps to keep in place the gap between the haves and the have-nots, and increasingly high prices for homes has made that intergenerational help even more necessary, making the gap between the haves and have-nots wider still.

* * *

AS MY HIGH school friends got ready for university, I was at a loss—I had no idea where I was going in life or what

I was going to do. I had, during previous summers (barring the time spent at the import-export job), worked at the law library at Toronto's York University. My mother had worked there as a secretary for a time, and the law librarian hired me to photocopy old books. The year I graduated from grade thirteen, I returned to that job, not knowing what I was going to do once the summer ended.

I am still haunted by the irony of it all: I thought of the university not as a place I could attend as a student but as a place at which I could work. Eventually, someone suggested that I could get a full-time job there. So I did. Once again, as a secretary.

I felt lucky—it was a good job, with benefits. And it opened my eyes to other possibilities too. Where I had previously had no expectation of furthering my education and getting myself in a position where I might one day make it into the middle class, accumulating wealth, or even owning a home—which opened up the further possibility of creating intergenerational wealth—suddenly that seemed more of a possibility. My benefits package included free tuition, and I began to take night courses. Professors I worked for—people I wouldn't have met otherwise—would ask me what I was doing here, knowing I could be something more than a secretary and wondering why I wasn't.

Sometimes, to get where you're hoping to be means being able to fit in as someone who belongs.

On Fitting In

"WHEN ARE YOU going to out yourself?" Eric Walters asks me. We'd had this conversation several times before. Both of us come from working-class backgrounds. We talked about outing and passing when we first met at a children's book conference—Walters is the author of almost a hundred titles—and returned to the subject whenever we met for a burger at the 1950s joint he'd gone to as a kid, right by the railroad tracks. It is in the same neighbourhood in which I now live; I've come here before with my daughter. It was recently razed almost to the ground, getting rid of sixty years of accumulated grease and grime, the memories of thousands of drunken 3 a.m. visits and first dates. It was rebuilt using the same footprint, the same neon sign and diner style—the new vinyl gives it a clean veneer, evoking nostalgia for something that doesn't exist anymore.

This time we're sitting, chatting on a sidewalk patio on a busy midtown thoroughfare in Toronto, a little east of the burger joint and those tracks that gave the area its name: the Junction. A series of railway lines, built where Indigenous trails once ran, create one of the biggest industrial crossroads in the city, home to both industry and the workers on which the industry depends.[58]

The streetcar rumbles past, occasionally drowning out our conversation. Here is where the 512 begins in the west end, the route looping at Gunns Road, the epicentre of the former industrial slaughterhouses that once dominated the area—the ghosts of which you can smell rising from the ground on a hot summer's day. There are still one or two small abattoirs, hidden amongst the mostly big box retail stores, craft breweries, and an incongruous subdivision of houses. Travel on into the working-class Old Weston Road neighbourhood, under rail tracks to Corso Italia, named for the wave of post-war immigrants who came to Canada for a chance to give their kids a better life. Families would buy a house and share it with two or three other families until they'd built up enough equity to buy their own place a little farther north, often in the industrial suburbs of Downsview and Weston, where semi-detached bungalows and backsplits gave way to factories and warehouses, workplaces and homes still close together. Someone once told me about a relative who got in trouble for keeping pigs in his backyard on the street where I now live. The area mirrors what we've done too: climbed from a tough, dirty past into a more gentrified life.

The streetcar continues on through Regal Heights and Wychwood Park, each block east representing a step up the socio-economic ladder. There are more detached houses. More three-storey duplexes. Bigger yards. A prettier aspect.

Along the way crossing Oakwood and later Vaughan—a few blocks apart on St. Clair, but angling so they intersect a little farther north in what the Toronto writer Zalika Reid-Benta describes in her book of short stories *Frying Plantain* as "the area where the Caribbean and Europe converged." Not a metaphor, she told me once, just a fact.

An area, she said, where "there would be a lot of Italian, a lot of Portuguese. But there would also be a very strong Island population . . . they sort of coexist. But they never really intermingle."[59]

Many of the kids here, who are Black, Portuguese, British, Italian, Asian, will go to the same schools, live outwardly similar lives while their lived experience is often quite different due to cultural traditions, income and class differences, gender and race and the intersectionality of any of those factors. As in any big city, diverse lives are being lived side by side, reinforcing the multicultural mosaic of which this country has so often been proud.

Crossing Bathurst into North Toronto—incomes and expectations increasing as the streetcar moves east—the community Facebook groups reflect certain assumptions about the world ("I want an excellent plumber who isn't expensive," "Our nanny is looking for a few hours' work on her days off," "I've got a great gardener if you're looking for one")—and then Forest Hill, where new money builds big houses. This is where the multi-millionaire hockey and basketball players and corporate presidents and politicians and media giants live. But there's only so much room. Not everyone will fit. Not everyone who wants to get there will, nor will everyone who deserves to. Not everyone knows how to. Not everyone even wants to.

The city leaves room for a multiplicity of lives.

Eric Walters and I are sitting on a patio in Corso Italia, a neighbourhood just east of Old Weston Road, the poorer part, now gentrifying, the part where Walters grew up with responsibilities no young kid should have to shoulder: his mother died when he was four years old; his father's mental illness would drive him to disappear for days at a time; his older sister left that toxic situation as soon as she could, and Walters had to fend for himself.

He became the "King of Jam Sandwiches"—also the title of his Governor General's Award–winning children's book. While his books for young people range in topic from math to the space race, it wasn't until he was older that he was able to write the one that finally won him that GG. *The King of Jam Sandwiches* is a novel, but it was *his* story: A book about class, about growing up in a neighbourhood with economic challenges, working-class, without many prospects. About the daily indignities of growing up poor—such as counting cans of food to see how long you might be able to feed yourself if your dad didn't come back and there was no money to buy more. And it was about wanting something more out of life.

He didn't write that book while he was young, he says, because "I wanted to get published." He wrote plenty of stories that editors *were* willing to publish and did—dozens of them. This story went unwritten as, instead, Walters did what most of us who are poor and ambitious do: he tried to fly under the radar and fit in. When he finally wrote a story about poor kids, he was told by an editor that the character wasn't believable. "He sounds too grown up," he recalls being told. Walters's reply? Of course he does—he'd had to grow up fast. To this editor, though, that translated into not being "relatable" for most kids.

But Walters' story isn't unusual. We try to fit in partly out of fear that people will decide that we don't belong, that we're outsiders, the them to their us—and we don't have the power to influence the decision. When belonging includes people in positions of power who determine whether you can get a job or whether your book is going to get published, then fitting in matters.

What gets lost as a result is authenticity and the complexity of our experiences.

* * *

TO THIS DAY, Walters still counts cans in his pantry. It's a childhood habit, and habits learned that early in life can have a powerful effect on how you move through the world, how you see it. Learning to fit in or conform—whether it's to the requirements of a classroom or a job or social group to which you wish to belong, or whether it's to grow within the community that you're already a part of—is something that begins from a young age.

First published in 1969 and updated ten years later, Melvin L. Kohn's seminal book *Class and Conformity: A Study in Values* demonstrated the connection between social class and values. He found, among other things, that parents from lower classes were more likely to emphasize the importance of conformity in their children, while middle-class parents were more likely to emphasize creativity and self-reliance.

He found that a parent's profession matters: those whose jobs allowed them more autonomy at work, whose work involved complex tasks and real variety (generally professionals or those who went to university), emphasized the value of self-direction to their children, while those whose jobs required a higher degree of following directives from other people (non-managerial, generally with lower levels of education) emphasized conformity, encouraging their children to be obedient and to fit in.

They encouraged behaviours that would have an impact on how their children conducted themselves in the workplace, and the long-term implications to these differing approaches have only served to perpetuate current class boundaries and challenges.

The impact parental status had on their offspring was also noted by the Organization for Economic Cooperation and Development (OECD) in its 2019 report *Changing the Odds for Vulnerable Children*.[60]

It takes, on average, between four and five generations, or "up to 150 years," for a child born into a low-income family to reach the average level of income.

Here's why: "As young people, they are likely to enter the labour market at an earlier age than their peers and take up low-skilled jobs at a time when technological change and globalisation are increasing the returns to education." This means that untrained and low-skilled workers fall further behind. In addition, the report says, low-skilled workers don't get as many opportunities to increase their skills or retrain. "Only 20% participate in job-related adult learning compared to 37% and 58% of medium and high-skilled workers."[61]

As technology changes and there are fewer chances for low-skilled workers to adapt and retrain, people who might have had to quit school to help support their family, or who weren't able to finish school for some other reason, are left further behind. The gaps in inequality widen, the report continues: "Already the political consequences of such dynamics can be seen in many countries, expressed through citizens' distrust of institutions and an overriding sense of discontent with the deal they have been given."

* * *

DAPPLED SUNLIGHT REFLECTS off the water as a canoe bisects the frame. Two grandparents, played by Katharine Hepburn and Henry Fonda, talk about growing old as their daughter (played by Jane Fonda, Henry's real-life daughter), and her son come to stay. A pastoral setting of middle-class life, even as it embraces the drama of coming of age, divorce, and aging.

It's an image that an early-teenage James Grainger absorbed. He lived in the inner suburbs and had recently moved to what he saw as a better area—still residing in a small brick apartment building, but in an area filled with bungalows and single-family homes. In the evening he would walk in his neighbourhood, looking in the windows of the families and imagining what their lives were like. They were the homes of the kids he went to school with. They were the ones his teacher seemed to have in mind when, one day, she screened the movie *On Golden Pond*.

When the film was over, Grainger recalls, the teacher sparked a discussion, asking the students to talk about how it felt the first time they remembered going to the cottage, cabin, or lake, and the first time they go each year. "And everyone has had this experience except me," says Grainger, who recalls feeling alienated and hurt. He didn't want to feel like an outsider in the classroom, and so "you know, you keep your mouth shut." It helps avoid feelings of shame, which can sometimes turn into feelings of anger.

For many students, it also means they don't participate in class, they keep quiet.

Grainger's teacher could have talked about the multi-generational aspects of the film, which might have been relatable to a wider range of children and encouraged a variety of stories. She could have talked about shared experiences with grandparents, which might have left out fewer kids, or perhaps of parents being divorced. She chose instead to talk about an experience many would see as privileged, one she assumed was the norm in the class she was teaching.

It adds to what Grainger calls "the defeatist psychology of growing up in the lower classes. You don't know how to negotiate that [more privileged] world. You don't have the cultural capital." The message is that you're not capable of fitting in, that you're in a different league than the more affluent or privileged people around you. So you silence yourself. The alienation Grainger experienced stuck with him for years.

When mobility is predicated on having shared experiences that give you an understanding of how to move within those worlds, how to fit in in those worlds, then you're at a disadvantage.

"I was eighteen years old before I spoke to someone who went to university who wasn't one of my teachers, my doctor, or my dentist," Grainger says. To someone who didn't have power over him but who was, rather, someone like him.

If you don't even know that a door might be open for you, that there's a door at all, there's little hope of walking through it. Although if merit were measured by marks instead of money, getting to university might never have seemed a barrier at all.

* * *

"SO HOW DID you get to university?" It's a question those who grew up in poverty or in the lower classes often ask each other: given the barriers, if they got to university, there has to be a story.

People don't forgo university, Walters says, just because they can't afford the tuition and costs of university. It's about other costs, too: you have to buy groceries, maybe you want to have a car, even a cheap second-hand one.

"How do you go on seeing other people with things, and you don't have things?" he says. "There's also that anger that evolves where you get to a point where you realize how unfair life is . . . and then you're just angry. And the anger can consume you; it eats you up. You don't assume you can go further because you don't know anyone that's gone further. That's the thing, right? How do you get there?"

"How did you know you were going to go to university?" I ask.

"I just knew that I didn't want to be nothing. I saw what was around and I thought, 'I want more.' But I also had a realistic belief. I knew it wasn't fair; and I knew I'd have to work harder than everybody else."

Some of the people he grew up with went to jail. He recalls when, as a teenager—and a self-professed "smartass"—he got beaten up by police in total three times. The time he was beaten up "the worst" he says, was one night when he and a few of his friends were hanging out at a bus shelter "because we had no place to go."

"A police car rolls up and [a policeman] says 'All of you, move it.' So I get up as my three friends leave, and I move to the other side of the shelter. And the policeman said, 'What the fuck are you doing?' So I said, 'You told me to move it, you didn't say how far.' They beat the hell out of me."

They beat him up, he says, because they could. Because he was poor.

"What about being treated with dignity?" I ask.

"It wasn't even a concept," he says. "You expect you are going to be beaten up. You expected that people are going to spit on you, basically."

Eventually, he says, "I saw what was around, and I wanted more." And he realized that he had to get out of his neighbourhood in order to get what he wanted, and he did. "One of my best friends lives not far from where I was growing up. [Although we were friends again before he died in 2022,] Steven and I stopped spending time together when I was about twenty-one. I came down to a party here. Johnny S. was shooting up in the corner. That girl Nick was with was probably fifteen. And I can't be with these people. And so I detach[ed] myself from the neighbourhood very deliberately."

Walters worked in a Consumer's Distributing warehouse from four o'clock to midnight five days a week during his first degree. He felt he had something to prove and went on to get four degrees in all, working as he went to school.

The multi-tasking is something so many do in order to make it. Knight was a waitress and barista, juggling jobs. Grainger worked in a factory until a friend walked him through the university application and student loan systems. As we've seen, Toten worked as a waitress but had to quit when her grades dropped and she was in danger of losing her scholarships. I worked full-time, went to university part-time, then switched this around when I learned a grant would cover my tuition.

Walters continues with his story. About ten years later he gets a call from Steve. Steve says, "Hey, Ricky"—what they called Walters then—"I need to apologize to you." "Is this step seven or eight in that twelve-step program?" Walters asks. "Number nine [making amends]," Steve says. "Look, Steve, whatever you said, it doesn't matter. It's no big deal," Walters tells him. But Steve insisted: "When we were about eighteen, I said to you, 'Who the fuck do you think you are to get out of this neighbourhood. Why do you think you're better than us?'"

It hurt, and it was a hurt Walters said he had put away, remembering the pain only when Steve apologized. "But that's the attitude," he says. Who do you think you are?

Your community can propel you forward, either through support or the impetus to escape; but the fear of losing your community can also hold you back—it's difficult to feel as if you're growing away from something you're familiar with when you don't know how to navigate something new. And sometimes people within your community can surprise you and show you something different.

* * *

THE BASEMENT CORRIDOR in the apartment in which we lived after being evicted from subsidized housing regularly reverberated with the sounds of people knocking, pounding on doors. But this time, a neighbour was knocking on our own, and for a reason. I thought this neighbour might be asking me to babysit; he lived with his wife and infant daughter across the hall, in a small, two-bedroom apartment that mirrored ours. He was an intelligent, intellectually curious man; I remember him as serious, even earnest, although I don't know his background, whether he had an education, and these days don't recall his name.

Instead, he gave me a few books that were to have an enormous impact on me. The first was Flannery O'Connor's short story collection *Everything That Rises Must Converge*. My neighbour was a very pious man. Every Sunday he'd go to the Peoples Church, where he had some position of small authority; given that church's evangelical bent, Flannery O'Connor's brand of Catholicism might have been a bit much for him. That book is one of the few possessions I've managed to hang on to all these years despite our peripatetic life. I'd done plenty of reading, but this book was different. It was hardcover, first published in 1956, this edition in 1965, and so seemed old enough and of a high enough quality to be important. It was also probably my first real encounter, at age thirteen, with an adult book that was nothing like I'd ever read before—one that dealt with class and race and change and spirituality and pettiness in a voice you could hear inside your head well after you'd put it down. It was the first time I'd been given such an adult book by a person who assumed I was smart enough to get it, or at least be interested enough to read it.

He also gave me a book called *Organic Make-up* by Mary Gjerde. When we were out of shampoo, which was often because it was expensive and not always a priority on the shopping list—unlike fish fingers and cabbage and ground beef and eggs and, once, as a "treat," tinned shrimp in cheese sauce—I would use dish soap to wash my hair. We could rarely afford conditioner, and with curly hair that was horrific to try to comb through at the best of times I could never get out all the tangles. Once my hair became so knotted at the back I had to cut it—I can still hear the sound of the dull scissors sawing through the mass of matted hair—leaving a large, uneven patch on the back of my head I tried to hide with a ponytail.

Organic Make-up provided me with the possibility of dignity as a teenager. I learned about egg white facials and putting oil (preferably olive, it recommended, but that was a bit exotic—and expensive—for us) and lemon in my hair. Organic make-up has always been there for the poor, long before being eco-friendly became something trendy, and often aimed at the upper classes.

* * *

WHEN I WAS finishing university and sending out applications for jobs, the first thing I did was buy the clothes I thought I would need to fit in. These were the days of *Dress for Success*—an updated etiquette book aimed at the aspirational professional crowd. There was a shop in a nearby mall called Heritage House: it was expensive and symbolized good taste to me. Old money. Where one could buy the kind of outfit, I thought, that people who might get the kind of job I wanted wore (even if I wasn't sure exactly what that job was). Perhaps the clothes I wore would lead me to the kind of professional job that Mary Tyler Moore had: I bought a navy blue wool skirt and a slightly military–style cream chiffon blouse; I thought of it as a blouse that meant business.

The dignity and confidence that come from having a nice, clean outfit and good hygiene is immeasurable. There are programs for women without means entering the workforce—whether they're escaping abusive relationships, are new to the country, are re-entering the workforce, or are living in poverty—that provide access to outfits they can wear to an interview. One such organization is also called Dress for Success, and it has chapters across Canada and around the World, "helping women achieve economic independence."

The way we speak—the words we use and how we say them, our grammar and syntax—can also affect our prospects in the workplace. Corporate jargon or industry-specific lingo has always been a way to filter people out. This is the way one acts, those workplace conventions imply. Whether in the way one dresses, the way one talks, or even one's etiquette, the implication is that the rules are there, and if you can't navigate them, you just don't *fit*.

When class and other factors such as race or gender intersect, then the conventions can be even more exclusionary. Recent surveys, for example, show that in North America having an accent (particularly one identified as non-white) can have an impact on whether a person gets a promotion.[62] Language can alienate and differentiate. By standardizing language, so that there is a "correct" way for people to speak, rules that everyone follows, the intention may be towards better communication; but when the "correct" way to speak is with a certain accent and certain pronunciations, it's worth asking who's making the rules and who's being excluded by them.

It's easy to make someone feel less than, even if you say—even if you *believe*—that by standardizing certain things you're trying to include them. Diversity and inclusion committees are being set up in companies nationally and globally in order to question existing power structures so that people aren't being excluded based on accent or race or gender or sexuality.

* * *

WHEN I WENT to my first job interview at a television station, I overdressed. The women interviewing me dressed much more casually, some wearing jeans, while I looked like I was pretending to be a banker. A familiar sinking feeling settled in my gut: "Oh, no, I got it wrong. I should have worn something else." So I did something strange. I crossed my legs and slouched—trying to send out signals that I was really much more down-to-earth than I looked. I simply didn't know how to act. Second-guessing plagues. You miss the nuance of the rules and so don't feel confident enough to interpret them—it's tough to know when you're doing the right thing when you haven't had a hand in making the rules and there's no one to guide you.

It wasn't the first time I'd overdressed. At university I'd brought a briefcase to class. I wanted to look as if I belonged to the future I hoped for. The only other person who dressed the way I did was from a small town; she was determined, too, to look as if she had a right to a more prosperous future.

I'd look at rich girls with envy, in their ripped jeans and their casual clothing, and wonder how they pulled it off. I didn't envy their money; I envied their confidence. It wouldn't have dawned on me to wear torn or dirty clothes in an effort to simulate street-cred; it reminded me too much of my own experience wearing unclean or damaged clothing—growing up I only had one or two outfits because there was no money—an experience that shaped my instincts, which were now drawn to tailored, neat, professional clothes. Besides, their clothes were never the real thing: they lacked authenticity, no matter how hard they tried.

As Amanda Mull points out in a recent article in the

Atlantic, clothing has always been used to indicate status, going all the way back at least to ancient Egypt. These days, being able to buy a small item, a pair of earrings or a small wallet, redolent of the European elite, something perhaps with a "Made in France" label (whether or not it was actually made in China) "encourage[s] consumers to think of a new purchase as part of a centuries-long elite fashion lineage—and to feel as if they themselves are part of that lineage too, if only briefly."[63]

When I was younger, it was hard to give the finger to fashion. Instead, I would try to figure out ways to look as if I had more money than I did. I frequented factory outlets, charity shops, and used clothing emporia and looked for better quality clothing. A trick for thrifting: look for cashmere sweaters. A nice one over a shirt and a decent pair of pants or a skirt can get you through a business meeting without the need for a jacket, or it can take you to an academic soiree. When you look as if you fit in, it gives you one less thing to feel self-conscious about.

Though practised bargain hunters, we nevertheless often give ourselves away by bragging about our bargains and wearing them with pride. We can't seem to help ourselves. When I lived in the UK, I went to a thrift shop and got a (real) Giorgio Armani top for about six dollars—a local celebrity regularly donated her often unworn clothes. This one has a tag on the inside—"Giorgio Armani/Bureau De Presse/Paris"—a revelation: she didn't buy it, she was gifted it; the company hoped her name would be seen in a magazine in bold print and she'd be asked who she was wearing. I felt like a million bucks wearing that Armani top, even though it cost me less than a tenner. I delightfully bragged to a boyfriend at the time about another score I'd made: a silvery, lacy Yves Saint Laurent top purchased second-hand for maybe forty dollars. "So much for exclusivity," he said dryly.

Not everyone is brave enough to talk about their thrift finds publicly. Catherine Hernandez is an exception. While she's now a successful author and filmmaker—her book *Scarborough*, about the diverse Toronto suburb of the same name, was made into an award-winning movie—she was until a short time ago a working artist and single mom living paycheque to paycheque, or, as she tells me, from "handful of change to handful of change that you find in your pocket."

As she became more successful, she gained more media attention and was profiled in newspapers and magazines across the country, including *Toronto Life*,[64] in which she was happy to share that her dress for the film premiere of *Scarborough* was a rental and her shoes from National Thrift, "the best thrift store ever." She views her purchases as a statement: she buys from Black- or Indigenous-owned shops and second-hand shops whenever she can to cut down her environmental footprint. She shares her finds, including the designer names, like any bold-faced celebrity. As a person who now has cultural power, she normalizes this way of dressing and makes it aspirational: dressing well on a budget becomes a point of pride, not of shame. What's wrong with going to the ball in second-hand clothes?

Dressing well can be an act of resistance in other ways too.

Kerri Sakamoto, too, is an artist, writer, and filmmaker—part of the Asian American art collective Godzilla that was founded in the early 1990s in reaction to an art world that generally excluded Asians; they organized shows and tackled subjects including the AIDS crisis, institutional racism, and gender representation, and worked to raise the profiles of artists from the Asian community throughout the art world.

Sakamoto's own grandparents—she is Japanese Canadian—immigrated to Canada in the early part of the twentieth century to escape poverty. Though anti-Asian racism was common throughout Canada and North America, after Pearl Harbor it became more virulent, resulting in the establishment of Japanese internment camps, where more than 22,000 Japanese Canadians, including long-time citizens, were unjustly imprisoned.[65] Sakamoto's mother was among them, and during the time that she was interned in these camps she learned how to sew. When the war ended and she was released and had started a family, she used these skills to make clothes for her daughters. She would sew outfits, Sakamoto says "to look like they're expensive."

It became an act of resistance: where they might face discrimination because of their poverty, or because of their race combined with their poverty, Sakamoto's family made the decision to dress well, to reflect the way they wanted to be seen and treated.

"I think this is very common in lots of people's experience to dress well . . . that was how we were going to present ourselves, as a kind of resistance to how people might perceive us and treat us," Sakamoto says.

Where the clothes I thrifted might have made it easier for me to look as if I belonged to a higher social class, the intersection of other factors of identity still complicates things. A white woman wearing nice clothes might seem to fit in to the middle class no matter her true economic standing, but identity is rarely so simple: a poor white woman might fit in where a poor Black woman would have both classism and racism working against her.

"People have talked about them so separately in a way, but there are all these combinations of race, class, gender, sexuality," says Sakamoto. Class, she notes, cuts through all of them—no matter one's race, gender, or sexuality, one always still belongs to a certain class. Nevertheless, when incidents around race and gender combine with class it can bring into question your right to inhabit certain spaces.

Sakamoto gives an example. "My stepson is quite fair," she says. "My husband's brown. He's Latin American. And his ex-wife is British background. There were times when I was taking [my stepson] to [his private] school and the reaction was 'Is that your nanny'?"

"Class will only take you so far," Sakamoto says. "You can still be brought down."

You can still face barriers to rising in the first place.

* * *

"WHAT WE HAVEN'T talked about is how it feels," says actor Jo Vannicola. We'd recently seen each other at that book launch where the talk had turned to back-to-school shopping, and we had decided to continue the conversation. "When we talk about those feelings . . . what it feels like to not have what [other] people have, it hurts."

I think back to the first time I went grocery shopping after I left home. As I pushed my cart through the aisles I kept track of everything on a calculator. Bread. Tea. Milk. Pasta. Jars of sauce. Oatmeal. I'd enter the price to make sure I didn't go over the thirty dollars I'd allotted for groceries that week. Because if I did, I wouldn't have enough to pay my bills. There wasn't anyone to rescue me.

As an independent contractor and freelancer, Vannicola's finances are constantly fluctuating. They left home at fourteen to escape abuse[66] and, one time, were invited to a friend's place in the country for Christmas. "I remember thinking, I've got to pay for gas there and back, I have to bring food, I have to bring wine, I have to bring presents. And suddenly you're hundreds of dollars in."

A hundred dollars can buy you groceries for a week or two; if you're really stretched, you can feed yourself for a week on fifty bucks. Although it's not something you'd want to do regularly—that kind of budget won't provide you with proper nutrition—plenty of people do it, leading to health concerns,[67] and increasing inflation only makes that situation worse.

It's not something you talk about because you try to avoid the shame and embarrassment of having to admit you don't have enough money, that you can't participate in the same opportunities and experiences as your peers. And so the question becomes: What does it take to have those same experiences? If you have a job or are in a social situation where there are certain expectations of you, how are you supposed to deal with these additional pressures? You don't want to appear cheap, or as if you're snubbing the crowd. But playing the role that is expected of you can put you in harm's way and make the hole you have to dig yourself out of even deeper. Your friends might have no idea of the implications spending money on a night out will have on your budget, particularly when they are able to take for granted their own ability to participate.

And so you don't talk about these feelings or vulnerabilities, in part because you don't want to make other people uncomfortable. It's difficult to admit to others that "I'm not experiencing what you might be experiencing, or what you think or assume I'm experiencing." It was for this reason that I had a hard time starting that conversation at the book launch. In order to avoid drawing unwanted attention, and to avoid those familiar feelings of embarrassment or shame, we often say nothing at all.

"It's always difficult, because it isn't to say that somebody who has a corporate job or owns their own business and makes a lot of money should feel horrible for having that level of success," Vannicola says. "But it doesn't mean that the person who's not making that kind of money is less valuable or less hardworking."

They pause.

"It might be that what we really all think is that this shouldn't matter. It's our humanity that should matter."

On Voice

ON A SUNNY afternoon in early March 2020, just days before the country and world experienced its first Covid-19 lockdown, Julie Dabrusin, then the parliamentary secretary to the minister of Canadian heritage, was in a crowded conference room to introduce a panel entitled "Writing the Next Chapter: Investing in Canada's Creative Economy." She was there at the invitation of the co-sponsors of the talk, the Economic Club of Canada and the Association of Canadian Publishers.

We are here, she told the audience of publishing and business people,[68] to celebrate "the importance of telling Canadian stories," and the importance of the economy's cultural sector, which contributes $53 billion to the country's GDP, more than agriculture, forestry, and fishing combined. The cultural industries are a major driver of employment, responsible for more than 666,500 jobs in Canada, including jobs for writers and filmmakers and studios and the coffee shops and spin-off industries that serve them.

"We . . . know Canada's creators are facing many challenges," said Dabrusin, "[and] deserve to be paid their fair share and be remunerated fairly." She stressed the importance of Canadians, including young people, having access to a wide variety of Canadian "content": "I want my own children to read Canadian stories," she said.

It made sense, in this room, at this time, that she'd mention the importance of strong copyright and rightsholders laws. These are issues that John Degen, the executive director of the Writers' Union of Canada, has long been fighting for. He was on the panel along with two writers, Sylvia McNicoll and Amy Stuart, alongside publisher Sarah MacLachlan, then of House of Anansi Press.

When the panel moderator turned to McNicoll and asked to what she credited her "longevity as a writer," McNicoll gave an unexpected—and honest—answer: "I credit my longevity as a writer to always being able to accept less income."

When talking about an industry that brings $1.7 billion to the Ontario economy alone, her statement is shocking—but so are the numbers. "There's a class issue that we don't always talk about in writing and publishing, where you need to be able to afford this life," acknowledged Degen, who pointed out that the average annual income authors earn from their writing alone is around ten thousand dollars.

As a result, there will be voices and stories we won't and can't hear. "We are not going to hear from poor people," said McNicoll. They're too busy hustling multiple jobs, they're tired, they don't have the resources to buy the mental space to write. This means that the stories we do hear will be told by certain specific voices: those who can afford to tell stories, whether those stories are their own or others'. In later conversation with me, McNicoll noted she had been able to operate as a writer making less and less money because she had other jobs, and because she had a husband with a full-time job.

McNicoll pointed out that, while you often don't hear poor people telling their own stories, in their own words, you do still get stories *about* poor people. But those stories are often told from the point of view of those who haven't lived the life, who don't have lived experience being poor. The stories they tell are, she feels, either largely aspirational or cheerfully affirming, and only rarely grapple with what it means to be poor, with details about the struggles and joys, the daily grind of life.

"I guess sometimes when you're writing for the mainstream . . . people may not be ready for the edge of the truth," she says.

* * *

WHEN WE TALK about class in terms of voice, what we are talking about is whose stories and voices are heard—by the mainstream, by policy-makers, by those in power—and, by extension, whose voices will shape the wider cultural narrative and decide what it's going to be.

When it comes to publishing, some attempt has been made to understand who, exactly, decides which stories are going to be published and whose voices are going to be heard. A recent survey conducted by the Canadian book industry's trade magazine *Quill & Quire* showed that almost 77.7 percent of people employed in the Canadian industry are age forty or under and 84.1 percent are women. Only 12.8 percent of respondents identified as non-white. Compare these with figures from the 2021 Canadian census, which show 50 percent of the population identify as women, 48 percent are under the age of 40, and 27 percent identify as a visible minority—clearly there's an imbalance in representation in publishing.

In terms of income, a senior editor, someone who has a certain level of industry experience and who acquires the stories and books that eventually make their way to bookstore shelves, earns an average of $54,700 a year, which is not much if you need to live close to one of the centres of publishing, such as Toronto, say. The *Quill & Quire* survey did not measure household income, which might better reveal what class most acquiring editors are in and what other financial supports, whether it be a partner's income or family money, exist to support this work. Many people in publishing work second and third jobs to make ends meet, sometimes teaching as part of English or publishing programs, or taking on editing and ghost-writing projects on the side, making publishing a viable career option for them. And not just in this country: HarperCollins employees in the United States recently went on strike specifically for what they term "fair wages." The average salary of an employee at the company is US$55,000, with the lowest salary being US$45,000—not much if you're living in Manhattan.

As author Joanne Harris recently put it in the *Guardian*, "writing books has been the great joy of my life. I fear it's becoming a career for the elite few."[69] Or, as McNicoll put it, it becomes viable only for those who can afford to accept less and less revenue from their writing.

When we speak of those responsible for telling—or approving—stories in the film and television industries and on digital platforms such as Netflix, we're largely talking about the producers and financiers. In 2020 the film industry contributed, according to the Canadian Media Producers Association, $12.2 billion to the national economy while creating approximately 244,500 jobs.[70] The association's aspirations are lofty: "What unites a population of 36 million citizens, spread across 10 million square kilometres?" it asks on its website. "In large part, it is the stories we tell to one another and the world. Storytelling doesn't just advance our culture; it is our culture." Producers develop those stories, then pitch them to line up funding and distribution and broadcast opportunities—meaning once they decide which stories they think will fly, they must approach other levels of gatekeepers who will play a large role in deciding whether these stories will be funded and aired.

All of this is part of what Julie Dabrusin calls the creative industries. They help define our culture by deciding whose stories are going to be heard, and who is going to tell them. If these publishers and producers and distributors and broadcasters are the gatekeepers of culture, as a group they are still fairly homogenous. Yet they play an outsize role in determining the narrative of our culture and whose stories we see and hear. And what they need to do better is ensure that there is more variety—in terms of race, class, gender, or some intersection of those—in whose stories get heard, and who does the telling.

* * *

WHEN THE LAWYER and activist Kiké Roach was growing up, her father and mother would organize rallies against racism and poverty, advocating for human rights. They were community leaders, yes, but Roach says their approach allowed those who usually didn't have a voice to be heard.

"One of the things that they would do is when they had these rallies and demonstrations, they would get the workers to speak for themselves. One of their main objectives was to rally people to listen to their story. Not speak for them, not "empower" someone else, but rather just pay attention to the structural, systemic ways that people, opportunities, or human rights are being trampled on," she said.

This was happening during the 1970s and 1980s, a time when mostly working-class voices were banded together in the union movement, a time when Charles Roach fought for the rights of migrant workers, people seeking refugee status, and even for the right to become Canadian citizens without having to swear allegiance to the monarch[71]—all issues that are still being addressed by activists today. But these days, "we're not hearing these types of stories enough," Kiké says. She believes there's a cultural reason for this: "We are very much a culture of political dynasties. And that's right from the top." Canada's head of state is still a monarch, the King represented by the Governor General. "That is the most ingrained, conscious, and unconscious signal that is sent out to everyone in this country," she says. It is, "the most exclusionary hierarchy of all."

Convincing cultural gatekeepers of the value—and the business case—of telling stories that portray a world beyond the familiar or comfortable is a continual challenge. When actor and filmmaker Jo Vannicola is making a film, much like their current project about LGBTQ youth who were forced to leave home and ended up living on the streets, they're also trying to find ways of getting it funded and distributed. Their income is often as a result

quite precarious—a choice they make in order to tell the
stories they feel deserve to be told.

Many of the youth whose stories Vannicola is telling
escaped from small towns, from homes of various classes
where their sexuality or their gender identity wasn't
accepted. It's not the type of story the young people themselves are able to tell—they are too focused, Vannicola
points out, simply trying to make it through the day, to
maintain a little dignity—finding public washrooms, for
example, so they can keep clean. Vannicola is aware that
this places them in both a position of privilege and power,
and that they must be very careful with how they
proceed.

At the beginning of every new project, Vannicola
heeds a few reminders they'll need to keep in mind to tell
the story that they're setting out to tell. "I'm going to have
some hurdles here. I'm going to rub up against . . . judg-
ments and thoughts: who's going to want to watch this
movie? Who's going to want to fund this film?"

Those challenges, the self-doubt that gnaws at their
confidence, won't stop Vannicola from telling their subjects' stories. "Because I think it matters."

But like Roach or McNicoll, they have to be financially
able to accept less pay, either by having some other means
of income or having access to other sorts of support. Even
here, there is both privilege and sacrifice involved: privilege in having the ability to tell their story or to help other
people tell theirs, and sacrificing potentially better paying
work in order to get those stories told.

* * *

CATHERINE HERNANDEZ'S WORKING-AND-POVERTY-CLASS
stories have been a commercial success. While Hernandez grew up in what she describes as a middle-class
immigrant household ("I had braces," she says, adding her
family was "well off for an immigrant family") as a young
adult, she spent years as a single mother, opening a home
daycare in the Toronto suburb of Scarborough to earn a
living as she raised her daughter.

"I was making forty dollars per child per day," she says.
"And if that child doesn't come in because the parents all
of a sudden want to go on vacation or they're sick, that's
a day lost. Forty dollars doesn't seem like much to me
now," but back then the loss would leave her with a nervous feeling in her stomach that she wasn't able to
shake—the images of unpaid bills piling up in her head.

While she was running the daycare, she would make
use of the local community centre and some of its programs. There was one particular program geared toward
children from newborns to age five where she could bring
the kids to play. The program began at 10 a.m., which was
perfect for her purposes. However, Hernandez says, the
social workers who ran the program decided to change
the program to target fathers, and then changed the tim-
ing of the program to 1 p.m.

That was, Hernandez says, exactly the wrong time for
what the community needed. There was little doubt that
many fathers would want to bring their kids to play centres, but it would have to be before or after work—not at
1 p.m., in the middle of the day, when most fathers were
working and many of the smaller children were being set
down for their naps. The staff told Hernandez that the
decision had been made at the main office off-site, and

that there wasn't anything that they could do about it.

"I was livid," Hernandez recalls. "I thought to myself, no one is going to attend that . . . and because there's no demand, the program will shut down, they'll shrug their shoulders and say, 'See, the proof is in the pudding.'"

"When it comes to social work, it really is *social* work—you have to know your community." Local social programs, Hernandez explains, tend to be run by front-line workers—those who "basically have a degree in hard knocks." They know the local community and are able to serve that community well. However, they're managed by umbrella organizations, by people who aren't onsite, who don't truly listen to the community or know what they need. "You have these people in offices with their social work degree making decisions that show zero understanding of the community and what it needs," says Hernandez. These are the examples that inspired the fictional stories in her book, particularly in the character of Ms Hina, a social worker who wants to speak up and challenge her boss but is afraid of being fired.

"In art, I would really challenge the industry to allow people to speak for themselves," she says. She sets an example: in her latest book, *The Story of Us*, she writes about "a deep friendship between a Filipino PSW and her elderly, trans woman clients." To ensure she got the voice and details right, she hired readers from the Filipino and trans communities, whom she paid "handsomely" to act as sensitivity readers. Yes, she says, she's worked as a caregiver and, yes, she's Filipino. But, she says, the "class difference is huge" between herself, who was born here and has an "Acadian accent" and grew up middle-class, and a newly arrived Filipino who has come under the Live-In Caregiver Program.

"There are stories that are not mine to tell anymore," she tells me. "I've moved on from this class . . . and I can make money in other ways. Now it's time for someone else to be able to do this work."

Hearing directly from those affected by policies and programs can make a big difference to how others come to understand and support their needs. John Clarke remembers a United Auto Workers union meeting in Oshawa back in the late 1990s, shortly after the Ontario Works program for welfare recipients came into effect. The small city east of Toronto had for decades enjoyed an industrial boom, with high wages and well-paid, unionized jobs, employing around 23,000[72] people at its height in the 1980s.

The idea of social welfare is rooted in the idea of the poor house, notes Clarke, which was designed to stigmatize poverty. Characterizing people who needed social assistance in a negative light is what, in their book *Poor People's Movements: Why They Succeed, How They Fail*, Frances Fox Piven and Richard Cloward called "rituals of degradation"—which aimed to make people moral outcasts for not being able to find work or because they couldn't work, and which in turn made them amenable to "offer themselves to any employer on any terms."[73] They originally coined the phrase in 1971, but it was brought to the fore again when the Ontario Works program came into effect in 1997, a program which saw benefits for those on welfare slashed, increased surveillance of recipients, and support tied to "welfare work participation."

"It manifests itself in the shame and trauma people feel," Clarke says.

He was invited to give a talk to an Oshawa union local

about the welfare system at the time. He decided to bring another speaker with him, a woman who was herself on social assistance, to give her own presentation. The union leaders of that local, he says, understood the connection between keeping welfare rates low and keeping wages to a minimum level—if welfare payments are too high, the thinking goes, then people will opt to go on welfare rather than work, forcing companies to increase minimum wage as an incentive to attract workers. Welfare offers a safety net, sure, but Clarke recalled that workers at the time directed a lot of hostility toward people on welfare. "The leadership of the [union] local was convinced we were going to be attacked," he said. There was "so much hostility" from the workers on the line toward people on welfare. The workers didn't lead a privileged life, he says, but they all made a decent wage and did "a tough, nasty job working on an assembly line . . . their contempt and anger towards people on welfare was so strong."

But then the woman got up and told her story, about why she was on welfare. She set out, Clarke says, the reality of living as a single mother on social assistance, sharing the math on her income versus her expenses, and she stressed how being on welfare affected her children. "And her story was so compelling, and she was so articulate and unassuming that people were in tears," he said. The workers at the meeting "were so taken aback that they actually took up a collection . . . that was under the table so she didn't have to declare it to welfare. It was incredible."

She was from Oshawa, Clarke says, but getting to know someone who was in different circumstances was a gulf they'd never crossed. Even though she was from their community, they were unlikely to have otherwise known her story. She was othered: the "us and them" narrative was clearly in place; bridging it was simply a matter of hearing her speak.

* * *

KAREN HARRIS AND I share a birthday. We discover this as we sit down to an early dinner at Red Lobster. She lives in the same apartment building as my mother had; after my mother died, she would collect her mail and call me when it had piled up, before the bills and junk mail stopped coming.

Her parents divorced just as she finished high school. They sold the house they had in the country outside Peterborough, her mother came to Toronto to look for work, her father remarried, and his new wife didn't want her living with them. "She told me I could go to a shelter," Harris recalls. She tried staying at a friend's house in Peterborough "but his dad was a raging alcoholic" and "that didn't work out." By this time, her mother had begun to establish herself in the city—she'd acquired an apartment and a job at a medical lab—so Harris followed. She was seventeen, just out of high school, and her mother helped get her a job at the medical lab, a job she stayed in for the next decade.

During this time Harris had her first violent relationship, a boyfriend she was with for four years. Drinking had been part of the culture when she was a teenager—when the local kids would come out to their property in the country, her dad would buy them a case of beer. But during her twenties her drinking escalated and she got into a cycle of toxic, abusive relationships—the kind the neighbours phoned the police about, the kind with yelling and physical abuse. She doesn't paint herself as a victim; "I hit him too," she says. Still, she kept up work, switching jobs to become an office supplies buyer, trying sporadically to "get sober."

At thirty-six, she finally managed to quit the drink—and this time it stuck. "I've been sober for twenty-one years," she says.

But getting sober did not make her life immediately easier. She got sober when her boss was on maternity leave. When her boss came back, Harris says, she remembered the "old" Karen and "treated me as if I was still the way I was before." It was tense for everyone, so, she says, they "agreed to part ways." Her next job, which she once again kept for "about ten or twelve years," was working in a distribution centre.

Even during all of the really tough times, she has always worked, while acting as caregiver to her mother when she was sick and, then, to her aging aunt and uncle who lived in Peterborough.

Harris is very tiny. She is about five-foot-one and weighs about ninety pounds. The joints on her fingers and her elbows and knees are swollen; her limbs are bone thin. By 2016 she was experiencing health problems and was diagnosed with nontuberculous mycobacteria lung disease, for which she says she was given a course of triple antibiotics. At around the same time, her rheumatoid arthritis flared up. For the next three years, she went through treatments for both—from steroids to prednisone and antibiotics—leaving her without an appetite.

She left her job and applied for employment insurance so she could focus on her health and, since then, has been working seasonal jobs or collecting EI as she deals with her fluctuating health issues.

In 2020, she found a job at a large, well-known delivery company. During the pandemic, the company was declared an essential service—"I was given a letter just in case anyone stopped me so I could show I was on my way to work." The company made big promises, she says, of a full-time job with benefits; she was hired on with that expectation and even paid union dues. During that six months, while her health was holding up, she worked as much overtime as she could and saved as much as she could. But as the cut-off date for a permanent position approached, she and her colleagues were cut back to twenty-five hours a week, a threshold at which they no longer qualified for benefits and no longer had job security.

Her rheumatoid arthritis flared up again, and she went back on EI hoping to focus on her health—plus, on EI, her prescriptions were covered. Those payments ended in January 2022. Her savings add up to the $11,000 she has left in an RRSP, around $1,500 in a TFSA and a $2,500 overdraft. With no family to fall back on, no inheritance coming, she's on her own.

"I've always been the Energizer bunny, but I just can't do as much anymore," she said. While she'd had flare-ups before, she says, "I'm older. It doesn't seem to be going away. And it's painful." She's still on multiple medications a day and wondering how she's going to be able to afford them. Her doctor has suggested she apply for a provincial benefit, which covers the cost of prescription drugs and is means tested: how much you receive is determined by your income.

Meantime, she's trying to find whatever work her deteriorating health allows.

She recently found a part-time job that paid twenty dollars an hour—assembling bath and beauty products, standing in one spot all day, something difficult for her to do with her rheumatoid arthritis. "If I were at least moving, then it would be easier," she says. But she quickly stiffens up, she's in pain. She's asked to be moved to another department, distribution, so at least she'd be able to move a bit more, but HR didn't fulfill her request.

As a single person with no family, she has to rely on herself. "I'm a lone wolf, it's just me." She figures if she could get something part-time, twenty-five hours a week at twenty dollars an hour—or about two thousand dollars a month before taxes—she could squeak by. But "it would be really squeaky," she says.

Another option is the Ontario Disability Support Program, which pays $1,228 a month, and only recently has been tied to inflation. If she doesn't qualify, her only other fallback is to apply for Ontario Works (colloquially known as welfare). That financial assistance program pays single people $733 a month ($343 for basic needs and $390 for housing). While Ontario Disability recipients are allowed to make up to $1,000 a month without incurring reduced payments, with Ontario Works, you're allowed to earn up to $200 a month without your payments being reduced or clawed back.

"I mentioned to the worker that wouldn't even cover my rent," she says about the Ontario Works payment. "She told me I could go and stay in a hostel or in a rooming house."

Harris's options are limited: she's hoping, given her

health issues, to be eligible for the Ontario Disability program. But applying for those benefits is a time-consuming and uncertain process. As the CBC recently reported,[74] about half of people who apply for disability benefits are initially denied them and have to appeal. Harris is hoping that, even if she isn't initially approved, she will eventually qualify.

What if that doesn't happen? What will she do if the money runs out and she can't pay her rent?

"I'm staying positive," she says. "Something will come up."

The alternative doesn't bear thinking about; the loss of her home, her dignity, would be catastrophic. But it drives home the point of how precarious life can be. I didn't have an addiction or mental health issues to deal with, although at one time I experienced a period of clinical depression. I was lucky enough to have family support, a doctor who cared, and it didn't turn out to be chronic. I also managed to get an education. Although we shared a birthday, Karen and I didn't exactly share the same experience. But we did share something else: our stories.

"I don't understand why people feel so threatened by having to learn about a variety of different life experiences—and maybe care about them," says Jo Vannicola finally. "Most people are passive, which is part of the problem." It's easy to stay within your own community, not having to see how others live, not having to know hardships. And if you don't know those stories, you don't have to feel responsible for them.

That's one of the most powerful aspects of storytelling: when you hear first-hand, authentic voices from those who have experiences vastly different from your own, you become a part of the storyteller's world. Listening to a story like Harris's frames a perspective that allows you to see a different point of view, while making it difficult to turn your head away. Then, Vannicola says, you have to ask yourself: What are you going to do about it?

That's why authentic voices are so important. Once you've heard and understood different perspectives from another's point of view, it's impossible to forget them, to ignore them. They become a part of who you are. You become part of the narrative: there is no us and them—there's only us.

If we get more alternative voices into the mainstream, at least everyone stands a chance of being heard. As Vannicola says, "It breaks down that barrier between those who have and those who don't. And it makes people think differently. I think that's very challenging to people who think a certain way."

Who we hear from matters, the narrative they create matters, and that is often a function of those who have the power to amplify their stories and voices—or, equally, to choose *not* to hear them.

On Community

I ALWAYS TOOK extra care when making soup for the Hunger Patrol. There is something visceral and highly personal about making food at home, knowing it will go straight into the bellies of those who need a meal, its nourishment and warmth.

I'd buy chicken legs—backs attached—a bag of carrots, another of onions, along with a bunch of celery and a large tin of tomatoes for each pot, enough to feed around forty people. I'd add a bag of curly egg noodles, a can of chickpeas or white cannellini beans to provide extra protein, cover the chicken with water, and bring it to a boil, the comforting smell of soup filling my kitchen, the thick yellow fat floating to the top, glistening, full of lip-smacking flavour and extra calories.

When we—the entire family participated—were ready to head to the church to prepare the evening's delivery, I'd put tinfoil over the top of each pot, then the lid over that to make sure the soup didn't spill; I put the covered pots in a cooler to keep them stable and load them into the back of the car. At the church, we'd reheat it all and add industrial-sized tins of chicken noodle soup to make it go further. A local bakery donated day-old bread, and everyone at the church would work together to make sandwiches—often peanut butter and jam—to be handed out alongside a Styrofoam cup of soup.

David Burrows, the Anglican priest who established the Hunger Patrol (he's now retired and it's run by others), handed out the soup from the back of a van each week through late spring, summer, and fall, when there was less shelter space than during the winter, a few volunteers accompanying him, among them usually a burly guy just in case there was any trouble—sometimes the people who came for food had mental health or addiction problems. Burrows would also collect thick socks and sweaters and shirts throughout the week, giving them to those along his route who needed them.

We often see community in action when people gather together in parks, churches, and community centres to entertain, hold fundraising events or pancake breakfasts to support local charities, to help those in the community who are in need, to raise awareness. The kinds of events that politicians might hold or sponsor, or where they might simply show up in the hopes of a quick photo op to show they're among regular folk or to gauge the mood of what seem to be everyday, average people.

We saw community at work when we banged on our pots and pans to show support for our front-line workers—but also to show defiance against Covid-19 itself: we shall work together and overcome. While we joined together to make a loud noise, raising our voices to show appreciation, that action has long been associated with protest: in 1848 when French housewives protested high rents, unemployment, starvation wages;[75] in 2015, when Brazilians protested against president Dilma Rouseff amid the Petrobras oil company bribery scandal,[76] and, later, in 2020, when they protested the way president Jair Bolsonaro was handling the pandemic, they did so by making a very similar sort of racket.[77]

The Covid-19 pandemic came at a time when, in this country and around the world, people were raising voices in solidarity and showing defiance in increasingly frequent protests: from the Arab Spring and Occupy demonstrations to anti-government protests in Hong Kong and Iran and anti-Brexit protests in the UK, the 2010s were, as NPR dubbed it, "A Decade of Protests around the World."[78]

Those protest years have occurred alongside, as David Brooks wrote in the September 2021 issue of the *Atlantic*, a change in how we view politics and the way politics reflect society. "It used to be straightforward," Brooks explained. "You had the rich, who joined country clubs and voted Republican; the working class, who toiled in factories and voted Democratic; and, in between, the mass suburban middle class.[79]

"Suddenly, conservative parties across the West—the former champions of landed aristocracy—portrayed themselves as warriors for the working class," he continued. "And left-wing parties—once vehicles for proletarian revolt—were attacked as captives of the super-educated urban elite. These days, your education level and political values are as important as your income is."

There's been a shift in the voice and narrative of class and equality, too, with other thinkers and critics noting that those who aren't seen to have "made it" are feeling increasingly left behind by both society at large as well as the communities to which they once felt they belonged.

"Unrepresented and fragmented by identity, large parts of the working-class left have shrunk into abstention or turned in favour to hard-right parties that claim to speak for the 'losers of globalization,'" writes David Broder in the Summer 2021 issue of *Jacobin* magazine, which was devoted to "The Working Class."[80]

While all this has been going on, while the narrative about who is and is not an elite has changed, so, importantly, have voting patterns. In Norway, for example, Broder illustrates how, between 1957 and 2009, working-class support for leftist parties shrank, while support for the same parties increased among the middle and upper classes. The same was true in Denmark.[81] Those with less education or fewer professional designations, who were once much more likely to vote for left-wing parties, are now far less likely or willing to do so.

Feeling like they've been left behind by globalization, many members of the working class seem to think former US President Donald Trump is "more relatable" than Democratic leaders with more obvious blue-collar credentials, Broder argues in that same piece. All parties—right and left—have been perceived by the dispossessed as having been taken over by "the elite": the intellectual elite are understood to be dominating the left, with their focus on identity politics, while the "merchant elite"—those who made their money importing and exporting goods—now control the right. And so those who don't identify as being part of an elite, who might not see themselves as budding intellectuals or academics or who didn't have the financial or business backing to join the merchant elite, can still at least dream about one day getting rich, and someone like Trump, with his self-propagated bootstrap mythology, is understood to represent something attainable, something to which they, wherever it is they currently find themselves economically or socially, could aspire.

Anthropologist David Graeber pinpointed exactly how wedge issues have been used to divide people when he wrote his "Bullshit Jobs" article for *Strike! Magazine* in 2013.[82] "In our society, there seems a general rule that, the more obviously one's work benefits other people, the less one is likely to be paid for it . . . Say what you like about nurses, garbage collectors, or mechanics, it's obvious that were they to vanish in a puff of smoke, the results would be immediate and catastrophic."

Seven years before the pandemic, Graeber was identifying what we would come to describe as the important, essential jobs in our society, the ones we later paid tribute to by banging our pots and pans and for which was provided, for a while, at least, hero pay.

So what happened? Graeber writes that advances in technology did not lead to the fifteen-hour work week economist John Maynard Keynes predicted for everyone in Western capitalist society; instead, we've seen the massive ballooning of the "administrative" sector: jobs that include telemarketing, corporate law, human resources. In other words: jobs created in order to give people something to do. It feeds into "the feeling that work is a moral value in itself." And when work becomes linked to identity, it becomes equally linked to notions of class.

This, Graeber argues, "is one of the secret strengths of right-wing populism. It becomes easy to mobilize resentment against," he writes, "school teachers, or auto workers (and not, significantly, against the school administrators or auto industry managers who actually cause the problems) for their supposedly bloated wages and benefits."

As David Brooks put it, "Classes struggle not only up and down, against the richer and poorer groups on their own ladder, but against their partisan opposite across the ideological divide."[83] In other words, class is not just measured in terms of income but also in personal and community values and beliefs. No class is a monolith, and neither is any one community, no matter how you struggle to change the labels to fit the changing times.

Journalist David Goodhart, in an effort to explain the populist fears he believes led to a "leave" Brexit vote in the UK, coined the terms "Anywheres" and "Somewheres" to describe two types of people, based on rather unique ideas of values, identity, and community. "The value divides in British society that led to Brexit, and may now break up the United Kingdom, stem from the emergence in the past generation of two big value clusters: the educated, mobile people who see the world from 'Anywhere' and who value autonomy and fluidity, versus the more rooted, generally less well-educated people who see the world from 'Somewhere' and prioritise group attachments and security," he wrote.[84]

These ideas seem quite germane to the discussion we're having, hearkening back as they do to the still essential notions of nationhood and globalism. But they're useful only to a point. They become another way of defining a hierarchy that sets certain types of professions against others, rural people and interests against urban ones, reinforcing the very same "losers" of globalization that Broder mentioned. And, as writer Ting Zhang points out,[85] these new descriptors still adhere to traditional definitions of class: it's much easier for an Anywhere—usually educated and mobile—to become a Somewhere than it is for a Somewhere—usually poorly educated and less mobile—to become an Anywhere. The latter are relying on their own and other countries to allow mobility: visas can be tricky, borders aren't always easy to cross, education in one country isn't always seen as on a par with that of other countries, and acquiring the skills in demand in other countries can be expensive and difficult. Or, as Zang puts it, "anywheres can remain trapped as somewheres."

Either way, the same factors that affect class mobility are in play: access to education; public policy that restricts options for certain segments of the population (even though, theoretically, these restrictions are the same for everyone); and the need to leave your community to benefit from globalization. Another way of looking at it is: Somewheres can be trapped as Anywheres if they're forced to leave their communities for opportunities even when they don't want to. No wonder so many people are feeling disenfranchised.

* * *

MEGHAN BELL AND I are having a few technical glitches over Zoom. When we finally get it right, I can see her sitting on a sofa in her living room in Vancouver. It's the middle of the pandemic, she's a new mother and happy to be able to meet with someone, even virtually, and chat like a grown-up.

"It's probably harder to find people who grew up rich and are willing to admit it," says Bell, as I explain this project. It was an interesting and unexpected perspective: that people who grew up rich might feel shame or embarrassment for their privilege, might not open up so much to avoid exposing themselves to judgment.

Bell's family is part of the .01 percent, the elite of the elite. Her family's business employs seven hundred people, whom they pay decently (but they could pay more), and they run their business ethically, as far as she can tell. Her maternal grandfather founded and grew the company her father eventually took over. In a 2019 article for *The Walrus*, she called for a wealth tax on families like hers, given rising inequality. She wrote:

> While I am grateful for the financial resources my parents have invested in me, I want a more equitable world, one where every child is cared for and has the opportunity to nurture their talents. Bluntly, it is incomprehensible to me that we live in a country where some people have indoor swimming pools and others do not even have clean drinking water.

She tells me that, "my issue is the level of inequality, and the fact that many people in essential jobs can barely make ends meet while other people have more money than they know what to do with." Bell has often criticized wealth, her family's included, "while benefitting immensely from it" in many ways; she was able to go to school with no student loans, for example, and later to buy a home.

She didn't pursue wealth as an adult: she chose to work in the arts, though she understood it wouldn't pay well; she married "a guy from a lower income family" who had a significant student loan and credit card debt when they got together, a guy who works for one of the local health authorities, mostly with people with addictions. "I wanted to do something that I felt was socially positive," she says. "A lot of people have to cave and sell out," she says, doing a job they don't want to. "It's a marker of my privilege that I never had to." Now that she's a mother, she's able to freelance part-time.

But even growing up within a wealthy family doesn't provide guarantees—and class is complicated. Most families, she points out, have branches that are working-class, some even poor. She refers to stories her husband has told her about the people with addictions he works with. A "significant minority" of them, she says, come from affluent families but need to access free community resources because they don't have a high income themselves nor good relationships with their families, making them functionally lower class.

"That's where I think the class conversation becomes very, very complex," she says.

* * *

FAMILY STORIES OFTEN change as each new generation understands their history differently and old stories are lost; community stories can become lost, too, as new generations look to new interpretations of the past. At the same time, older stories can be rediscovered, allowing us to look from another perspective at where we came from. An example of this is the story of the Tolpuddle Martyrs, which was forgotten in the mid-nineteenth century, their influence being rediscovered years later and now celebrated.

We are all, with the exception of Indigenous people, immigrants to this country. Successive generations have come to Canada for a variety of reasons—to escape colonialism, persecution, poverty, war. No one immigrant story is the same, although there are touchstones of shared experience: each involves leaving the communities in which they were born, creating a life in a new country. There is a complexity to these stories informed by an intersection of factors, including race, gender, sexuality, and class.

Sakamoto, for example, when we talk, is working on a project that focuses on a wealthy Korean family and explores inter-ethnic Asian dynamics and class. She's approaching it in the context of the current environment of global capital and migrations, she says, an environment which has changed immigration patterns and led to great class differences; in particular, she says, it has led to, within the Asian community in the U.S, the largest difference between income levels of any racial category[86].

This project, she says, is trying to explore that intersection of class, race and experience.

She points to her own family's experience as an example: Her grandparents immigrated in the early part of the 20th century because they were poor and hopeful of finding a better life. This is the story her own family grew up with: that their forebears were "peasant stock."

These days, many Asian immigrants coming to Canada are much wealthier than their forebears, and are immigrating for different reasons, to educate their children, for example.[87] "They have totally different historical experiences, different migratory histories." The needs and perspectives of older and perhaps poorer parts of a given

Asian community aren't the same as those of newer immigrants with more money.

There's a culture gap between different waves of immigrants, even within families, where the first generation was poor and the next generations more prosperous. "I think the new reality is that class and race are bundled up together."

* * *

IN SOME WAYS this is a position that journalist and activist Desmond Cole echoes, in the sense that the Black community contains a multiplicity of class experiences. He is the author of the 2020 book *The Skin We're In: A Year of Black Resistance and Power*. "We don't have to have these polarized discussions about race versus class, because we are all living a different set of experiences," he tells me. Some people within the community might become lawyers, or chiefs of police, or, like himself, someone with visibility within the community, but that doesn't tell the whole story of the Black community.

"Whatever visibility and so-called success that we may enjoy within Canadian social life," Cole says, "is not representative of what is happening for the average Black person. And we have to actually consider what's happening for the average Black person in this country. We're not all going to grow up to be judges, and police officers and lawyers and corrections officers and politicians. And I don't think we need to aspire to these things in order to demand a good life."

While he says that a powerful activist community such as Black Lives Matter has the potential to galvanize the fight for equality, he also points out that different communities can work together in solidarity to achieve things, while still recognizing and honouring their differences. "In the ideal, we can unite and express solidarity with, for example, disability justice movements, joining with racial movements, joining with labour movements, jumping [in] with people who are fighting for queer and trans rights," he says. There is often the suggestion, he says that, unlike race, class has more power to unify: "that 99 percent versus the 1 percent narrative that most of us are not the elite; we are not the rich and powerful [and] there is a much broader solidarity to be had if we forget about race and simply unite along the basis that we are the 99 percent."

But that discussion, he believes, downplays the idea of solidarity. He offers the following example: he was doing outreach in parks in downtown Toronto, where people living in tents were being removed by police. The parks, he asserts, are public places and "homeowners and condo owners around these parks would like to have these spaces all to themselves." Cole says he might have more in common with the condo owner, in "that none of us are the elite." "But they [those condo owners] are not showing solidarity with those in their own communities who are suffering the most," he says.

"We have to accept that there is a great deal of Canadian society right now that, if it is not rich and powerful and wealthy, would like to project that onto itself . . . would rather relate to those elites than to those struggling in their own communities."

Solidarity is the same word that trade unionists such as John Clarke or Bryan Evans use—solidarity is what we were embracing with the pandemic cries that we're all in this together.

No community is a monolith and it's dangerous to see things that way. The qualities that bring communities together—shared experiences, shared histories, shared values—are also the issues that drive us apart. Understanding each other, within our own communities and listening to the experiences of people in other communities, is the thing that will bring us together.

Beyond the Hero Narrative

"I've heard, 'We went from being heroes to zeroes,' and that's exactly how a lot of us have felt."
　—Andrew Spielman, Calgary grocery store worker[88]

"Once called heroes, now we're zeroes, right?"
　　—Rafal Fratczak, registered practical nurse.[89]

"JUST REMEMBER THIS, Mr Potter. That this rabble you're talking about . . . they do most of the working and paying and living and dying in this community. Well, is it too much to have them work and pay and live and die in a couple of decent rooms and a bath? Anyway, my father didn't think so, people were human beings to him. But to you, a warped, frustrated old man, they're cattle. Well in my book, my father died a much richer man than you'll ever be." So said George Bailey as cooperative banking and capitalism met in one of Hollywood's most emotional moments.

Whatever the flaws with Frank Capra's now classic 1946 movie *It's a Wonderful Life*, it airs every December around the holiday season when we're vulnerable to ideas of hope and goodwill and mutual generosity. We are vulnerable to thinking that those of different classes are equally worthy of living lives of dignity. Maybe that's why I seek it out every year. George wasn't an obvious hero. His younger brother, Harry, was the more conventional one, coming back from World War II decorated for his bravery; his friend Sam Wainwright, too, part of the newly confident industrial complex, making good by getting in on the ground floor of plastics. But George Bailey still resonates; his long slog sticking up for the little guy, his point of view on the world that cost him dearly financially and almost drove him mad, all made him one of most complex film characters ever to appear on the big screen.

The movie wasn't particularly popular at the box office despite garnering a raft of Oscar nominations. It became a holiday season staple only when, in the 1970s, copyright protection ended, its owners failed to renew it, and it could be aired by television stations without paying any royalties[90]—an ironic turn given its underlying message.

* * *

THE SWISS CHALET on Laval Drive in Oshawa is surprisingly uncrowded for five thirty on a Friday evening in June, the usual phalanx of families with little kids busy doing something else, leaving older couples out for an early dinner to fill the few occupied tables in the dining room. Waiting in a booth in a quiet corner is Sherry MacKinnon , a friend I hadn't seen since high school. I'd been following her story as a personal support worker on Facebook and contacted her to see if we could talk.

MacKinnon is a caregiver, like her mother before her and her daughter after her. Every day, she tends to her roster of clients, helping them wash, ensuring they're safe, providing conversation and company. She witnesses life and death and decline, and the everyday moments families don't have the time or, sometimes, the inclination to deal with.

She is one of the front-line workers we hailed as everyday heroes when the Covid-19 pandemic first broke out—the ones we banged on pots and pans to thank, understanding the importance of their work to keeping us alive, fed, and cared for.

"I didn't feel like I was a hero. It was, to me, my job," she says. It was "scary" in the beginning with new protocols and constant sanitizing and not knowing what the impact really was of Covid-19. "Nobody knew anything. It was just, we have this virus, we have to deal with it."

Some of the changes this new situation demanded were immediate: looking down the hallways at the retirement homes in which some of her clients lived, there were now towers full of PPE (personal protective equipment) outside of every room so she could fully change each time she came to look after these mostly elderly clients. Other clients—they ranged in age from as young as thirty to as long-lived as 102—resided in the community, at their own homes or with family; her daily visit allowed them to maintain their independence.

It's heavy, difficult work. She is often lifting people who are bedridden to shift clean sheets and absorbent pads under their bodies. She helps them to the shower and cleans them or helps them clean themselves, "always with dignity." She pays attention to whether they have eaten their food, or whether they are more or less alert than the day before. She pays particular attention to changes in their bodies so that she can alert a nurse if, for example, they develop bedsores, or a wound becomes septic.

Her official start time is 7 a.m., and her official end time 4 p.m.—but since some of her clients are in nursing homes and breakfast is at 7:30, she often starts at 6 a.m. to accommodate their schedules, although she doesn't get paid for the extra time.

During the pandemic, after every shift, MacKinnon would phone her partner at home and tell him to "get my robe ready." She'd get out of her car, walk up the stairs to the second-floor apartment they share in a six-plex, an apartment she loves—"I have two balconies, one at the front of the building and one at the back"—and, just outside the door, take off her work clothes. She'd put them in a plastic bag, then head to the shower to wash up, trying to ensure she didn't bring Covid into her home. When she did once, she took to her bedroom—which opened up onto one of the balconies—to self-isolate for the required ten days, which she was paid for because she contracted Covid from work. She considers herself lucky—other people she knows had to use vacation time.

She loves her job and her relationship with her clients and their health; she is frustrated at the lack of respect for PSWs within the health-care system.

"There are the doctors," she says, holding her hand above her head to show where doctors are in the hierarchy. "Then there are the nurses," she says, moving her hand down a few inches. She drops her hand almost level with the table. "And this is where PSWs rank," she says. "We are not seen as part of the 'interdisciplinary team.'"

This is the thing that bothers her most. The care she offers clients is among the most personal and intimate of all, yet her contribution is marginalized.

MacKinnon didn't plan on being a caregiver. When she was in her mid-forties she was laid off from her job at a local historical tourist attraction. At around the same time, her stepmother decided to do a course to become a personal support worker. MacKinnon hadn't finished high school, but her stepmother's example gave MacKinnon the courage to apply for the college program. "I was intimidated," she said—and wasn't even sure if she'd get in. She applied through a "second career" program, was accepted, and took the PSW training course—in-class and work placement over twenty-four weeks—finishing second in her class with a 94 percent average.

Wages vary for PSWs across the country. According to the Government of Canada's job bank, they earn a minimum of $13.50 an hour, rising to a maximum of $35 in more remote territories.[91] The "hero pay" they were given at the beginning of the pandemic, which ranged between an additional $2 and $3 an hour, made a difference. MacKinnon credits the Ontario Personal Support Workers Association for urging lawmakers to make that initially temporary top-up a permanent wage increase.

The OPSWA was created in 2010. While the exclamations about honouring pandemic heroes may only have seemed to be lip service, the association ensured that the workers' collective voices were really heard. When even collective voices aren't enough to effect change, the voices of those who are feeling the pain of not getting the services they need just might be. Personal Support Workers might be undervalued, but they're essential. As MacKinnon points out, being disrespected and underpaid makes people quit essential jobs. "People realize they don't have to work for peanuts." And so the voices being raised the loudest might be the voices of those who suffer when there's a shortage of PSWs—vulnerable people in need of care who aren't getting it.

As Dr Isaac Bogoch said, the pandemic presented a unique opportunity to highlight inequalities in housing and working conditions and the needs of marginalized populations. It also provided another opportunity: to understand how linked we all are, and how much we rely on each other's labour and sacrifice. Though the claims that "we're all in this together" sometimes sound trite, the challenges with health-care staffing shortages, needing workers to ensure we can access food, underscores our mutual dependency.

As we finish up our conversation in Swiss Chalet, McKinnon asks me, "So, are you going to be able to use my story in your book?"

"Of course," I say. "It's important."

* * *

IF WE HAIL people as heroes but treat them as second-class citizens, it raises the question: Who are we really talking about when we talk about heroes? When we bang our pots and pans, who are we banging them for? Do we mean people who move mountains? Those who do jobs that others don't want to do? Who go above and beyond and risk their lives so other people are safe? Who overcome poverty and lack of opportunity in order to create conventionally successful lives, moving at least into the middle class?

In the context of the pandemic, we brought our banging pans of appreciation together to honour a certain type
of hero: those who helped us by keeping us alive as we
were locked down. In this case, we define heroes as those
who help us, risking their own lives to do so. They serve
the broader community at their own individual risk.

When we talk about class, we often define heroes as
those who pull themselves up by their bootstraps, where a
poor person, through hard work and perseverance, escapes
an impoverished childhood and moves into a more prosperous life. The kind of hero that emerges in the bootstrap
narrative feeds into our society's foundational story of individualism, the sort of individualism that settled the
prairies. It implies that this is a land of opportunity if you
work hard enough, and if you're poor it's your own damn
fault. These stories serve to reinforce the myth that our
forebears came here and carved out a life for themselves:
but most were subsidized by government to settle here,
often by being given land stolen from Indigenous people.
Did they work hard, our forebears? Undoubtedly—but
they didn't do it entirely on their own. Hard work isn't
erased by support; the two aren't mutually exclusive.

The bootstrap narrative also reinforces the idea that a
person must fight to escape their lot in life: that we must
be constantly striving, wherever we may find ourselves,
however much we may already have, for more. Surely
there's more to heroism than that. But this belief ignores
the fact that not everyone wants to be a banker or a business person and money isn't the only way to measure merit.

What room does that leave for those who have stories
like MacKinnon's? She says she didn't feel like a hero, that
she was only doing her job. But we can't just dismiss who

she is and how she lives her life. It is heroic to do what she did, to do what is necessary under difficult circumstances, at increased personal risk. She deserves respect and dignity. But by not hearing and celebrating stories like hers, we don't give them credence: we undervalue them.

The Italian socialist Antonio Gramsci used the term "organic intellectuals" to describe people who are not educated in universities but who have organized, who have lifted themselves out of terrible circumstances—people who are smart and who in public debates can often "wipe the floor" intellectually with people who had all the benefits of wealth and privilege, Ontario Coalition of Poverty cofounder John Clarke tells me. They emerge in poor and working-class communities and are "incredibly important people but totally undervalued."

Figures like the Tolpuddle Martyrs might be included in that list. More recent names might also include, Clarke says, J.B. McLaughlin, who came from the coal fields in Scotland and ended up leading miners' struggles in Cape Breton. Or Jeannie Campbell, who, Clarke says, came from a working-class Glasgow background, became a postal worker leader in London, Ontario, and played an essential role in trade union struggles. "There are so many people who've [come out of] public housing," he says, "lifted themselves out from under circumstances that were incredibly challenging."

But amongst the working-class, he says, "there's much less understanding of the people who have made a contribution within and for the interests of working-class people. Not many can name the people that played a big role in building unions, or people that helped to organize the unemployed during the Great Depression to survive.

Again, there are quite towering figures that I would say were certainly on par with any of these upwardly mobile champions."

Their achievements tend to be collective, not individual. Perhaps that's why we don't see them. Or perhaps because they don't fit into the narrative of upward mobility that underscores the narrative of the American dream or the Canadian good life, their stories stay marginalized.

That doesn't mean they are any less heroic. Their lives and stories are as important a part of our history as the big historical figures we usually read about, and their lives show that there is a different way to live, one that centres dignity and compassion.

* * *

THERE ARE NO conventional heroes in author Kevin Hardcastle's books. In his review of Hardcastle's 2015 collection of short stories, *Debris*, Robert Wiersema described the settings—rural small towns and countryside—as "a world that may appear as foreign as any imagined science-fiction or fantasy milieu." These locations "form a world of desperation, violence, poverty, and helplessness populated by thieves and police officers, door-to-door salesmen and factory workers."[92]

Don't get me wrong, there are protagonists in Hardcastle's stories, who often go to what we might call heroic lengths to do what needs doing—but not in the manner of the bootstrap narrative. These are ordinary people, poor people, trying to get by and trying to build a life for themselves. And there is a quiet heroism in this.

Class has always been central to Hardcastle's personal

narrative; his father was born in Liverpool, his mother in Northern Ireland. They moved to rural Ontario, where Hardcastle was born and raised. The stories he writes are about the rural poor— something he knows all about.

"People don't like my books because they say nothing happens," he tells me in an interview. In *Debris* and in his 2017 novel, *In the Cage*, his characters are simply leading their lives, nothing happening being part of the point. Dealing with class in fiction, he says, is all about how characters are represented, how they are portrayed.

He talks about his own family and how his parents, as working-class immigrants from England, had gone to a small town and had to integrate and "figure out how they were going to fit in. Maybe that also made them more open or accepting to other people in that community who were marginalized." They were, after all, trying to carve out or build a life for themselves and encourage their kids to do the same.

It's these types of stories, the stories of ordinary people living ordinary lives, that don't usually get told. His parents were poor, which meant growing up that the power would get cut off when there wasn't money to pay the bill, there might not be any hot water. He hated Christmas, he recalls, because "if we ever got anything good, I think, *What did it cost them to get it?*"

These are the details of poverty—details that aren't always included in stories without being idealized or used as a metaphor or a device or to victimize the characters. If stories about the lives of ordinary people aren't told authentically, how are we going to understand what's really going on in people's lives without them becoming untextured and two-dimensional?

And if these stories aren't being told, how are lawmakers and policymakers to understand lives they haven't
experienced themselves? We don't get change—we get a
reinforcement of a specific set of values. In this milieu,
where can change possibly come from?

Conclusion

WHAT STRUCK ME as I've been writing this book is that the stories are both urgent and timeless. The experiences I had in grade school echo in the experiences of poor students during the pandemic: a lack of decent housing, a lack of resources for educational necessities (books in my day, accessing the internet and computers now). The issues are the same; only the specifics have changed. Yet these immediate concerns and necessities have an impact on the future people can aspire to.

As I wrote for the *Toronto Star* in 2022,[93] overall inflation hiked prices for the usual range of goods including gas, clothing, and housing by 8.1 percent in June—a level not seen in forty years—recovering slightly to 7.6 percent in July and 7 percent in August. Food inflation rose even more sharply, to 10.8 percent in August, according to Statistics Canada. In March of 2022, 160,000 people in Toronto visited food banks—rising from just 60,000 in March 2019—according to the Daily Bread Food Bank. Six months later, that number had risen to 182,000 people—a 170 percent increase in visits from before the pandemic.[94]

The last time inflation was that high was in the 1990s, when it hit 12.47 percent and, before that, in the 1970s, when it hit 11 percent.[95] Thanks to a series of interest rate hikes, inflation finished the year in Canada at a year-long average of 6.8 percent.

The suggested solutions offered to people who are suffering as a result of inflation is generally the same as it has always been: cut your spending accordingly and take personal responsibility for your well-being. But as valuable as this advice may seem on first glance, it also does two things. First, it reinforces the false narrative of individual responsibility: if you can't succeed, even in a time of scarcity, then it's your own fault. Second, it raises the question: If your spending is already cut to the bone, what more are you supposed to do?

We've been here before. When inflation in the US spiked to more than 12 percent in the 1970s (spurred largely by rising energy prices), then-president Gerald Ford sanctioned the "Whip Inflation Now"—or WIN—campaign. It had at its core an appeal to individuals to help wrangle inflation under control by both spending less and using less energy.

As Michael Grasso explained in *Jacobin* magazine, while the campaign did little to actually bring down inflation "WIN did demonstrate that, within the living memory of Ford's core of GI Generation voters, there was a powerful abiding memory of what it meant for an entire country to believe (or at least be *persuaded* to believe) we were all in this together. Governmental efforts to encourage thrift, especially on energy, popped up in the Carter administration [1977 to 1981], again from a place of shared responsibility."[96]

As Grasso goes on to point out, the rhetoric of collective action was very powerful, and people got behind the scheme, "even if the reality of these programs was wholly meant to protect the capitalist class" by placing responsibility for the economy squarely back on individuals and not on the systemic issues that had caused the crisis in the first place. But then as now, we need to ask ourselves: Are we really all in this together? And if we are all in this together, if responsibility for our current and future well-being is shared, who is then responsible for inequality? And what can we do to ensure that there is less of it?

For those who weren't born into privilege, who don't have a post-secondary education, a fall-back, a safety net, there's no margin for error, and the consequences of any mistake can be massive. Without family to call on, people like Karen Harris are on their own financially: there's no forthcoming inheritance, no one to help if a job is lost or an unexpected expense comes up. For some families that means that a child could be left without food or school supplies, an older person left increasingly isolated and struggling to keep the lights on, a person with health problems losing their home and dignity.

Perhaps the most important takeaway from all that I've heard and seen is that inequality isn't good for anybody. But I've also seen that the world can be reimagined as one that centres well-being and dignity if we listen to each other, like those GM workers listened to the single mother in their community. Well-being and dignity aren't reflected only in income: they are realized in access to education, food security, decent housing, safety. For Lise Hewak, it means being able to take a minimum wage job and be treated with respect. Or for Sherry MacKinnon, it's to be treated as an integral part of the health-care team so that she can better meet their mutual patients' needs.

We all deserve respect and dignity.

It's encouraging when business scions point out some of these key issues, as happened when food magnate Michael McCain announced that he was stepping down from the helm of Maple Leaf Foods in 2022. "The fundamental drivers of food insecurity [are] not food," he told the *Globe and Mail*. "Canada has an ample supply of food ... It's all of those systemic issues that are at the core of food insecurity,"[97] he said, "which include income inequality, poverty, mental illness, access to skills (including financial and nutritional skills) and racism."

There are times that it can feel as if the voices raised in concern about class issues and inequality simply aren't being heard—but that's putting the onus for making themselves heard on those with the least power. Not everyone is doing better. Inequality is growing. It's getting more and more difficult to stay in the middle class. And inequality isn't any better for the upper classes than those at the lower end of the spectrum. Inequality isn't good for anybody.

"This is where I'm feeling that my success actually perpetuates a system that's wrong," says the writer Eric Walters. "Because I am an example of somebody being able to make it."

He compares it to going to a casino: the odds are stacked in favour of the house. But in order to keep customers coming back for more, there have to be occasional winners. "There's got to be enough success that the system looks like it's got some fairness to it, that you can win," he says. "So the few of us who do win are the example that the system isn't completely rigged. And it is rigged."

It's time to change the narrative to reflect that. It's time we all embrace the idea of truly being in this together and make this a society that works not just for an elite few, but for everyone.

* * *

IN MID-MARCH, 2022, I take the five stairs down to the front door of a yellow-brick apartment building in Toronto. It stands three storeys high, with each floor holding about eight units. Some of the people who live in those units work in various jobs—in the deli at the local supermarket, at a medical clinic, in the film industry— while some are retired, living on their pension income, or, like Karen Harris, who lives in this building, trying to get by with various jobs in a gig economy, juggling precarious employment.

In a few months, the balcony above the entrance will be festooned with hanging flower baskets—the tenant there creates a screen of bright blossoms, providing a cooling screen as well as a burst of colour, that thrive in the south-facing sun during the dog days of summer. Summer music will escape from inside—the beating bass of classic rock or the acoustic guitar of 1970s folk drowning out the sound of cars rushing past on the main street. Most of the units have balconies, except the ones in the basement, but the basement is where I'm headed, to the first unit on the right. In the lobby, footsteps echo off the old terrazzo floors.

When I open the locked glass door, reinforced with wire mesh to safeguard against shattering, and enter the hallway, I hear the clink and scratch of the washers and dryers—the laundry room door stands open a few doors down from my mother's unit. She died in early March, and I need to clean out her apartment. Fluorescent lights reflect a harsh shine off the hallway's floor, and the smell of fabric softener sheets sends a warm perfume wafting throughout the building.

Those units that face east look out on a patch of lawn and trees, screening the off-ramp from the Gardiner Expressway; at least there's green there, and privacy, even if the debris blown up from the highway covers the windowsills and curtains with a dark grit—the apartments facing west or north look out onto the driveway or parking lot. Inside, the smell of dust rises from the once-green curtains I'd put up for her when she moved in, the material no longer feeling silky but permeated with dirt.

The rents aren't high, although they're not consistent throughout the building; if you were lucky enough to move in before they really started to skyrocket in 2018, when the provincial government took rent control off new buildings, sending rents skyward, and landlords with older buildings tried to get more rent through "renovictions"— where tenants could be asked to move while renovations were done, and landlords could raise the post-renovation rent substantially—you could pay as little as $850 for a one-bedroom unit without a balcony. A new company bought the building from the private owners about five years previously and began repairs through attrition: as tenants moved out, they'd upgrade the suites and charge as much as $1,750 for a revamped unit, changing the demographic of who could afford these apartments or further squeezing tight budgets (overall in Ontario, between 2017 and 2021, food bank visits increased by 32 percent,[98] in keeping with the trend of rents increasing over the same period).

The new owners wanted to make a good first impression to those prospective new tenants. They had tried to gussy up the lobby a bit by adding a graphic paint job of sharp-lined grays and blacks, bringing the decor from the 1960s into the 1980s, wiping out the pastel painted mural of a slightly tropical summer scene, putting fake plants in the now-dry trough of a once-gurgling water feature that had stopped working long ago.

In the older suites where tenants had lived, some of them, for thirty years, the new management didn't undertake repairs or upgrades unless absolutely necessary. These units were stuck in time, with mismatched green and pink heavy porcelain bathroom fixtures; missing tiles patched with whatever was on hand. In my mother's unit, kitchen cabinet doors were falling off their hinges and a musty smell escaped from under the kitchen sink. Countertops showed the knife marks of decades of chopping vegetables without a cutting board, and chipped doorframes revealed, like an archaeological dig, layer after layer of tenants' attempts to beautify their tiny homes. I had wanted to put an air conditioner in the unit so my mother could have some relief in the summer, but she was nervous about the dated wiring, so I couldn't. Neither could I set her up with a microwave. Quick meals are a godsend for most seniors, but the microwave would trip a fuse so we had to take it away, too.

Still, independence was important to her and, here, she could shut the door on the rest of the world; not be bothered by the sights and sounds and smells and concerns of other people's lives and judgment. Depending on how you measure luck, she was lucky: in her mid-eight-ies, she was able to maintain her independence despite her age and her most self-destructive proclivities, mostly because she had children who would bring her food if she needed it, do her taxes, make sure she had a phone. Other older and vulnerable people without means during the pandemic weren't so lucky. People living in nursing or seniors' homes, for example, accounted for 80 percent of all Covid-related deaths in the pandemic's first wave.[99] My old friend Sherry MacKinnon shook her head as we spoke about them: "Those poor souls."

When my mother died, I phoned the landlord to give him notice—he changed the locks and wouldn't let me in because "I don't know who you are and what she's got hidden in there," he said. My brother and I consulted a lawyer, but before we had to start writing letters I was given a key and the directive to "scrub the walls." When I got in, I immediately spotted evidence of others having been there before me: an open window to let in the fresh April air; some of the wood parquet floor tiles already taken up—finally being replaced after years of loose buckling—done now with the knowledge they could finally charge a higher rent for the renovated unit. Some vanilla-flavoured Ensure I'd bought her and left on the counter before we took her to the hospital were gone.

"Why would they do that?" a friend asked me when I told her.

"Because that's how they treat poor people," I said.

The fear poor people live with has a lot to do with it. The worry that they'll be kicked out of their place and be in the position of having to find something new. They don't necessarily know how to push back, and if they do, they worry they're going to lose their affordable rent, their home. When you are consistently facing precariousness—whether in a job or in housing, you—we—learn not to make a fuss; it can be a hard habit to break, and we put up with behaviour that is sometimes illegal. In this case, I was in management's eyes an extension of my mother, deserving of the same treatment. Even though I was in a position where I could have sicced a lawyer on them—the rent was paid up to the end of the month and they had no right to access the apartment except when we permitted them to do so—there was no indication anything else had disappeared and at that point I just wanted the place cleared out. I was already grieving, trying to decide how I was going to remember my mother; hers was no longer the type of life I lived, and I neither wanted to have to feint and deke and fight every move the property manager made or deal with it for any longer than I had to. Companies like the ones that own my mother's building count on capitulation: but where my mother couldn't afford to walk away, I could, for better or for worse. That, now, was my privilege. I didn't have the energy to hold the company to account, and I wasn't interested in playing a game where the manager was creating the rules—I left the dirty walls for him to figure out.

Rocking the boat still makes me afraid, in the pit of my stomach, that everything will come crashing down. After years of mostly just looking for a workaround for situations like this instead of calling others to account, it's hard to be more proactive. If you don't even know when it's possible to speak up, second-guessing also becomes part of who you are.

Sometimes I get angry too: what if all the hard work and energy I'd expended had gone into something useful instead of fighting? Fighting to bootstrap your way into a better situation might seem heroic, but it's a drain of time and talent. And it seems a losing battle anyway: I might be equally talented as someone who had a more privi-leged start, but I'd always be trying to make up lost ground. I also never quite feel as if I'm on solid ground; I know how quickly things can change, my peripatetic life as a child drummed that lesson into the very core of my being: that someone else's decisions, a change in circum-stance, or bad luck could change everything. That's true for everyone; perhaps the real difference is our confi-dence in ourselves, in our abilities, in the system we're living with, and in our own futures.

I had managed, through a combination of luck and hard work, to shed the "stickiness" that the OECD and economist Miles Corak noted plagued the bottom 10 per-cent of income earners and became, instead, part of the top 10 percent.[100] My family growing up would either have been in that bottom 10 percent, the group of fami-lies least likely to experience upward class mobility, or at least in the bottom 40 percent, where insecurity prevails and whose children are as likely to move upward as downward. Part of the groups for which it seems that, as the EKOS survey suggests, the middle-class agreement, the agreement that engendered a feeling that working hard and playing by all the rules would get you some-where, would set your family on a steady path, has been eroded. Now, that same survey found, the feeling is, even though "I worked hard [and] played by all the rules . . . there's not much I can do (to) guarantee my children a better lifestyle than me." We are left with the feeling that class mobility is little more than "the luck of the draw."

I walked back up those five steps, went to my car. I turned left out of the potholed driveway and drove back into a life that was different from the one being lived by the people in the yellow brick apartment building, vastly different from the one in which I had grown up, a life that a combination of luck, government policy, and hard work now afforded me.

In some ways, it would be easy to keep on driving and not look back. But I take on board something Jo Vannicola said: once you know people's stories, you can't forget them. We become responsible for each other by knowing each other. I've got a foot in both worlds, and it's important for those who can bridge worlds to do so.

It's not always been comfortable talking about class; it's not been comfortable "outing" myself as Eric Walters put it. But by doing so, other people opened up and talked about their individual experiences and ideas and thoughts about class and the various realities that intersect it too. Even during the most difficult conversations, though, we all listened. There have been so many times, like at that cocktail party, where there were opportunities to start a conversation about class—and when we did, most people were eager to take part.

Once the conversation has started, it's important to keep it going, to create spaces that centre respect and dignity. We're all in this together, after all.

Acknowledgements

THIS BOOK BEGAN as a conversation. Dan Wells—the owner of the independent publishing house Biblioasis in Windsor, Ontario—and I would often talk about our working-class and lower-class upbringings. When Wells conceived a series of books titled Field Notes, modelled on the tradition of pamphleteering, we both thought class would be a perfect subject. Thanks, Dan.

The book is meant to start a conversation, and conversations are at its core. Thanks to Meghan Bell, John Clarke, Desmond Cole, Miles Corak, Bryan Evans, James Grainger, Kevin Hardcastle, Karen Harris, Catherine Hernandez, Lise Hewak, Chelene Knight, Sherry MacKinnon, Sylvia McNicoll, Kiké Roach, Kerri Sakamoto, Teresa Toten, Jo Vannicola, and Eric Walters for taking the time to talk with me and being so excited about some of those conversations being reproduced in this book.

Thanks to my King's MFA mentors David Hayes and Ken McGoogan for reading and rereading drafts, and for their encouragement, positivity, and support. Thanks to everyone in the King's program for the chances to read for an audience, for the feedback, and for always being there to talk—I'm looking at you, Melanie Chambers.

Thanks to Scott Sellers for his ear and advice and decades of friendship. Thanks to Sarah Murdoch, Sue Carter, Janice Biehn and Elena Angeloni for early reading and feedback; to my Emery Friends Group, Maria Latham, Victoria Mackin, and Michelle Klein for being there and understanding all the postponed plans.

Thanks to Rachel Ironstone for copy editing and Emily Mernin and Vanessa Stauffer at Biblioasis for their work on publicity and getting this book through production and to print. Thanks to my colleagues at the *Star* for their encouragement, Tess Kalinowski, Brian Bradley, Julie Carl. And thanks to so many others I haven't named for conversations, recommendations, and leads that I was able to follow up.

And, mostly, thanks to my family. To my brother: Andy, we made it through. To my dad for his endless encouragement—he might not have known how to get us there, but he always wanted something better for us. To my husband, Patrick McCormick, and daughter, Abby, for their dinner-making, housework-doing, and endless patience and support that freed me up to do this: I love you both.

Class is a big subject. This book is only about thirty-five thousand words. Inevitably, some perspectives were left out or given less space than others. Certain anecdotes or studies did a lot of heavy lifting in the narrative because they were rich in depth and breadth, allowing me to at least touch on an idea, a reason, a cause. For those who feel strongly about something I haven't mentioned, let's talk about it. That's the point.

Finally, writers can't always be saved from themselves, their mistakes, and their misquotes, despite an editor's best efforts. And so, in the tradition of authors everywhere, I note that any inaccuracies that remain are mine.

Endnotes

1 Patty Winsa, "Pay Premiums for Grocery Store Workers Have Ended. Did Their Essential Status Change? Labour Rights Advocates Say No," *Toronto Star*, June 16, 2021.

2 Kaeli Conforti, "How To Work Remotely in the Bahamas for up to One Year," *Forbes*, December 19, 2020.

3 Laura Begley Bloom, "Want to Live and Work in Paradise? 7 Countries Inviting Americans to Move Abroad," *Forbes*, July 30, 2020.

4 Geoffrey Morrison, "Estonia's Digital Nomad Visa Now Available," *Forbes*, August 12, 2020.

5 Bloom, "Want to Live and Work in Paradise?"

6 "Working from Home During the Covid-19 Pandemic, April 2020 to June 2021," Statistics Canada, August 4, 2021.

7 Thomas Lemieux, et al., "Initial Impacts of the Covid-19 Pandemic on the Canadian Labour Market," Canadian Labour Economics Forum, Working Paper Series, Spring-Summer 2020, WP#26.

8 "Province Doubles Support for Parents With New Ontario Covid-19 Child Benefit," Ontario Newsroom, News Release, March 31, 2021.

9 Aaron Wherry, "One Country, Two Pandemics: What Covid-19 Reveals about Inequality in Canada," CBC News, June 13, 2020.

10 Ibid.

11 Lemiuex et al., "Initial Impacts of the Covid-19 Pandemic."

12 Sheila Block, "Racialized and Indigenous Workers Are Bearing the Brunt of Pandemic Job Loss," *The Monitor*, January 14, 2021.

13 David Cannadine, "Introduction" of *The Rise and Fall of Class in Britain* (New York: Columbia University Press, 2000).

14 Bernard de Mandeville, "The Fable of the Bees," as cited in Karl Marx, "Chapter Twenty-Five: The General Law of Capitalist Accumulation," *Capital, Volume I*, reproduced online at Marxists.org.

15 A Global News report notes that, in the 2019 Federal election, "The four main party leaders have mentioned the term middle class nearly 100 times on the campaign trail, and the Liberals reference them term 48 times in their 85-page platform." Andrew Russell, "Who Is Canada's Middle Class and Why Experts Hate the Term," Global News, October 10, 2019.

16 OECD, *Under Pressure: The Squeezed Middle Class* (Paris: OECD Publishing, 2019).

17 Ibid., 19. It is noted that class refers to people who share "the same socio-economic status" and that is measured in different ways depending on discipline,

usually using employment occupation or income. In chapters three and four of that same OECD report, job polarization and consumption is analyzed—"in either case, the middle-income class remains the benchmark," Ibid., 21.

18 Ibid., 28.

19 "Through a Lens Darkly: Shifting Public Outlook on the Economy and Social Class," EKOS Politics, October 10, 2017.

20 Ibid., 2.

21 Christo Aivalis, "Trudeau's 'Middle Class Tax Cut' Is a Sham," *Canadian Dimension*, February 24, 2020.

22 "What Does a Minister of Middle Class Prosperity Do? Mona Fortier on Her New Job," interview by Laura Lynch, *The Current*, CBC, November 22, 2019.

23 "Through a Lens Darkly," EKOS Politics.

24 Ibid.

25 Unifor Local 598, "Our History," minemill598.com.

26 René Morissette, "Unionization in Canada, 1981 to 2022," Statistics Canada: Economic and Social Reports, November 23, 2022.

27 "Trade union density rate, 1997 to 2021," Statistics Canada: Quality of Employment in Canada, May 30, 2022.

28 Rosa Saba, "After Years of Decline, the Percentage of Unionized Workers Is Increasing Again—and the Pandemic Is Likely the Reason," *Toronto Star*, Feb. 12, 2022.

29 David Olive, "Our Last Good Premier? How Bill Davis Nearly Quadrupled Ontario's GDP and Created the Province We Know Today," *Toronto Star*, August 13, 2021.

30 Tracy Smith-Carrier, "Low Funding for Universities Puts Students at Risk for Cycles of Poverty, Especially in the Wake of Covid-19," *The Conversation*, October 18, 2020.

31 OECD, *A Broken Social Elevator? How to Promote Social Mobility* (Paris: OECD Publishing, 2018), 5.

32 Ibid.

33 Miles Corak, "Chasing the Same Dream, Climbing Different Ladders: Economic Mobility in the United States and Canada," Pew Research Economic Mobility Project, January 12, 2010.

34 OECD, *A Broken Social Elevator?*, 5.

35 Ibid.

36 Ibid., 18.

37 Rosa Saba (@RosaJsaba), "Millions of working Canadians saw their incomes devastated by the pandemic—but thanks to millions in bonuses, Canada's top execs did just fine," Twitter, August 18, 2021, 10:38 a.m.

38 Rosa Saba, "Dozens of Canadian Companies Quietly Tweaked Formulas to Make Sure CEOs Still Got Their Bonuses During the Pandemic, Report Finds," *Toronto Star*, August 18, 2021.

39 Lawrence Mishel and Julia Wolfe, "CEO Compensation Has Grown 940% Since 1978," Economic Policy Institute, August 14, 2019.

40 Abigail Johnson Hess, "In 2020, Top CEOs Earned 351 Times More than the Typical Worker," CNBC, September 15, 2021.

41 Oxfam measured a surge in billionaires "alongside the erosion of individual corporate tax rates and workers' rights and wages." In "A deadly virus: 5 shocking facts about global extreme inequality," Oxfam International online.

42 James Tapper, "Rich Countries That Let Inequality Run Rampant Make Citizens Unhappy, Study Finds," *The Guardian*, April 17, 2022; the primary source for this piece is David Bartram, "Does inequality exacerbate status

anxiety among higher earners? A longitudinal evaluation," *International Journal of Comparative Sociology* Volume 63, no. 1 (May 2022). DOI: 10.1177/00207152221094815.

43 Quotations in this section are from Government of Canada, "Opportunity for All: Canada's First Poverty Reduction Strategy," canada.ca.

44 Statistics Canada, Table 13-10-0834-01, "Food Insecurity by Economic Family Type," released March 23, 2022.

45 Edward Dunsworth, "The Transnational Making of Ontario Tobacco Labour, 1925–1990," PhD thesis, University of Toronto, 2019, 2.

46 Jamie Bradburn, "The 1960s Backlash over the Minimum Wage," TVO Today, January 22, 2018.

47 Dunsworth, "The Transnational Making of Ontario Tobacco Labour," figure 2.5, 133.

48 Numerous studies suggest that there is profiling in both the education and police systems, including Scot Wortley and Maria Jung, "Racial Disparity in Arrests and Charges: An Analysis of Arrest and Charge Data from the Toronto Police Service," Ontario Human Rights Commission, July 2020.

49 Cynthia Kumah, Jessica Rizk, and Rachel Smith, "Beyond the Classroom: The Future of Post-Secondary Education Has Arrived," Conference Board of Canada, March 3, 2022.

50 Students would buy textbooks from local bookstores such as Squibb's in Toronto, which reported taking a hit to the business when the province started buying the books instead in the early 1990s. Jackie Hong, "Squibb's Stationers celebrates 90 years in Weston Village," *Toronto Star*, May 4, 2017.

51 Up to the 1950s, Black train porters were treated differently from whites, who were in unions that negotiated only on behalf of white workers, and who could be promoted. Travis Tomchuk, "Black Sleeping Car Porters: The Struggle for Black Labour Rights on Canada's Railways," The Canadian Museum of Human Rights, February 27, 2014.

52 That attitude appears to have prevailed even during the Covid-19 pandemic. An auditor general's report on inspections of migrant farm workers' lodgings by Employment and Social Development Canada showed that workers weren't given adequate lodgings to ensure health and safety. In an interview with CBC News, Syed Hussan, an executive director of Migrant Workers Alliance for Change, said that the agency "was not created to protect migrant farm workers. It was created to ensure a steady supply of cheap labour." John Paul Tasker, "In Scathing Report, Auditor General Says Feds Failed to Protect Foreign Farm Workers from the Pandemic," CBC News, December 9, 2021.

53 Jeremy Seabrook, "Why Shame Is the Most Dominant Feature of Modern Poverty," *The Guardian*, September 30, 2014.

54 The Canadian Press, "Home Ownership a Priority to Millennials: Poll," Global News, March 25, 2016.

55 Chris Fox, "More than 40 Per Cent of Young Homeowners in Ontario Got Financial Help from Parents: Poll," CTV News, February 22, 2022.

56 Gary Mason, "The Great Generational Wealth Transfer Is Under Way," *Globe and Mail*, March 12, 2021.

57 Keith Costello, "The 'Great' Wealth Transfer: An Opportunity or Threat?" *Investment Executive*, October 11, 2016.

58 "Junction Triangle Railway Railpath, Early Years," Toronto History, Heritage Toronto.

59 Deborah Dundas, "Zalika Reid-Benta's Debut Book Puts Midtown Toronto on the Page at Last," *Toronto Star*, June 7, 2019.

60 *Changing the Odds for Vulnerable Children*, OECD Library, November 19, 2019, DOI: 10.1787/a2e8796c-en.

61 Ibid., 5.

62 Aysa Gray, "The Bias of 'Professionalism' Standards," *Stanford Social Innovation Review*, June 4, 2019.

63 Amanda Mull, "Fashion's Racism and Classism Are Finally Out of Style," *The Atlantic*, July 7, 2020.

64 Courtney Shea, "'There are Scarboroughs all over the world": A Q&A with Writer Catherine Hernandez, Whose Film about Toronto's Most Notorious Suburb Is Sweeping TIFF," *Toronto Life*, September 16, 2021.

65 "Government Apologizes to Japanese Canadians in 1988," CBC Archives online, posted September 22, 2018.

66 Vannicola wrote about their upbringing in their memoir *All We Knew But Couldn't Say* (Toronto: Dundurn Press, 2019).

67 "What Are the Implications of Food Insecurity for Health and Health Care?" PROOF: Food Insecurity Policy Research, University of Toronto.

68 A full video recording of the panel is available on the Economic Club of Canada's Facebook page, dated March 5, 2020.

69 Joanne Harris, "Horribly low pay is pushing out my fellow authors—and yes, that really does matter," by *The Guardian*, December 7, 2022.

70 "Our Industry," Canadian Media Producers Association (CMPA) online.

71 Jeff Green, "Charles Roach, Toronto Lawyer and Human Rights Advocate, Dies at 79," *Toronto Star*, October 3, 2012.

72 Jeremiah Rodriguez, "General Motors' Oshawa Assembly Plant: A Brief History," CTV News, November 26, 2018.

73 As quoted in Krystle Maki, "Neoliberal Deviants and Surveillance: Welfare Recipients under the Watchful Eye of Ontario Works," *A Global Surveillance and Society?* 9, no. 1/2 (November 30, 2011).

74 Erik White, "Ontario Disability Support Rejections Often Overturned on Appeal by Provincially-funded Legal Clinics," CBC News, February 25, 2019.

75 Nicole Narea, "Why Protestors Have Been Banging Pots and Pans outside Their Windows," *Vox*, June 5, 2020.

76 Andrew DeSimone, "Brazil's Pots and Pans Clamor for Progress," *Forbes*, March 30, 2015.

77 "Coronavirus: Brazil Demonstrators Bang on Pots and Pans," BBC News, March 19, 2020.

78 Claire Harbage and Hannah Bloch, "The 2010s: A Decade of Protests around the World," NPR, December 31, 2019.

79 David Brooks, "How the Bobos Broke America," *The Atlantic*, September 2021.

80 David Broder, "The Many Farewells to the Working Class," *Jacobin*, Issue 42, 30.

81 A Canadian study published in 2022 in the *Canadian Journal of Political Science* found "a clear and distinct trend where the working class has increased its support for the Conservatives." There is still support for the NDP, the traditional party of unions and the working class, but the study found that the party had added support from other classes "diluting the class-based support of its electorate." Matthew Polacko, Simon Kiss, and Peter Graefe, "The Changing Nature of Class Voting in Canada, 1965–2019," *Canadian Journal of Political Science* 55, no. 3 (September 2022), 663–686.

82 David Graeber, "On the Phenomenon of Bullshit Jobs: A Work Rant," *Strike! Magazine* 3 (August 2013), later expanded into the book *Bullshit Jobs: A Theory*.

83 Brooks, "How The Bobos Broke America."

84 David Goodhart, "Why I Left My Liberal London Tribe," *The Financial Times*, March 17, 2017.

85 Ting Zhang, "The 'Somewheres' vs. the 'Anywheres': It's Not Just a Political Divide," *Medium*, April 8, 2020. The article features a subhead that indicates the divide is both economic and systemic as well.

86 Rakesh Kochhar and Anthony Cilluffo, "Income Inequality in the U.S. Is Rising Most Rapidly Among Asians," Pew Research Center, Washington, D.C. (July 12, 2018) https://www.pewresearch.org/social-trends/2018/07/12/income-inequality-in-the-u-s-is-rising-most-rapidly-among-asians/

87 Frances Bula, "Wealthy Chinese Immigrants Come for Better Housing, Not Money: Study," Frances Bula, *Globe and Mail*, September. 5, 2016.

88 Marlene Habib, "Why Grocery Store Workers Remain the Unsung Heroes of the Pandemic," *Globe and Mail*, July 13, 2021.

89 Gord Howard, "Niagara health-care workers say they're burned out, angry over lack of support," *Toronto Star*, July 22, 2021.

90 Branden C. Potter, "Why 'It's A Wonderful Life' Was a Box Office Failure," *Grunge*, April 9, 2021.

91 "Personal Support Worker—Home Support in Canada," Job Bank, Trend Analysis online, last updated November 16, 2022.

92 Robert Wiersema, "Review: *Debris* by Kevin Hardcastle," *Quill and Quire*, November 2015.

93 Deborah Dundas, "Thanksgiving Should Also Be about Dignity. Let's Share Our Collective Bounty," *Toronto Star*, October 10, 2022.

94 Ibid.

95 "Canada Inflation Rate 1960–2023," Macrotrends.net. Data sourced from the World Bank.

96 Michael Grasso, "Whip Inflation Now," *Jacobin* 46 (September 27, 2022), 51.

97 Ann Hui, "Canada Is Facing a 'Terrible' Food Crisis, Says Maple Leaf CEO Michael McCain," *Globe and Mail*, May 24, 2022.

98 "Hunger Report 2021: How the Pandemic Accelerated the Income and Affordability Crisis in Ontario," Feed Ontario research report, November 29, 2021.

99 Janine Clarke, "Impacts of the COVID-19 Pandemic in Nursing and Residential Care Facilities in Canada," Statistics Canada, June 10, 2021.

100 The top 10 percent of earners earned a minimum of $96,000 per year. Pamela Heaven, "Posthaste: Canada's Top 10% of Earners Pay 54% of Taxes—But Here's the Kicker, Many Are Just Middle Class," *Financial Post*, January 23, 2020.

DEBORAH DUNDAS grew up poor in the west end of Toronto. She is now a writer and journalist, has worked as a television producer, and is currently an editor at the *Toronto Star*. Her work has appeared in numerous publications in Canada, the UK and Ireland, including *Maclean's*, the *Globe and Mail*, the *National Post*, *Canadian Notes and Queries*, the *Belfast Telegraph* and the *Sunday Independent*. She attended York University for English and Political Science and has an MFA in Creative Nonfiction from the University of King's College. She lives in Toronto with her husband and daughter and their loving, grumpy cat Jumper.